Mastering Variable Surface Tracking

The Component Training Approach Workbook

Ed Presnall

Dogwise Publishing
Wenatchee, Washington U.S.A.
www.dogwise.com

Mastering Variable Surface Tracking: The Component Training Approach Workbook
Ed Presnall

Published by
Dogwise Publishing
A Division of Direct Book Service, Inc.
403 South Mission Street
Wenatchee, Washington 98801
509-663-9115
www.dogwisepublishing.com
info@dogwisepublishing.com

Editing by Barb Steward

Cataloging-in-Publication Data is available upon request from the Library of Congress.

ISBN 1-929242-12-3
ISBN 1-929242-13-1 (Book and Workbook Set)

Printed in U.S.A.

Table of Contents

Legend of Component Symbols

01	**Component**	Component Number for reference use
	Start	Start flag or position of start
	Article	Article position
	Transition	Transition area
	Surface Change	Change of Surface
	Automobile	Automobile
	Building	Buildings and Structures
	Garage	Garages and Open Buildings
	Wall/Fence	Walls, Fences and/or Hedges
	Elevation	Elevation - berms, landscaping, etc.
	Ramp/Stairs	Ramps, stairs
	Water	Standing or Flowing Water
	Alley	Alley or Walkway
	Curb/Gutter	Curbs and/or Gutters

Beginning Training

For the purposes of this lesson plan, we will assume that your dog has a basic understanding of tracking. In my training program, I routinely incorporate all of the lesson plans into the training program for a TD level dog.

The object of the **Basic Training Lesson Plans** is to introduce your dog to contaminated areas, transitions, starts and non-vegetated surfaces through the use of simple, easy-to-lay tracks. Utilizing a local park, business park, campus or church you should be able to locate sufficient space and acceptable terrain to accomplish these plans. Be creative when evaluating potential tracking locations. You are not searching for a single location where you can lay multiple test-length tracks, but rather are evaluating multiple sites where you can lay multiple component tracks ranging from 150 to 250 yards each.

Each exercise as presented will incorporate an overview page, sample track diagrams and a sample worksheet showing the example tracks in a *simulated* environment. It is recommended that you print the pages encompassing the lesson plan you will be working on as well as several blank **Tracking Notes** pages to allow you to plot your tracks and accumulate a workbook of your training tracks. These training tracks or Tracking Notes pages will allow you to follow and evaluate your dog's performance and note any weak areas you may identify which will require additional training. These sample tracks are <u>examples only</u> and should be modified to fit into your available training location.

There is no set timeframe for the execution of these lesson plans. I normally train three days a week, year around, and am comfortable in completing all of the **Basic Lessons** in under six-weeks. That said, your mileage may vary and your timeframe may be extended based on your training schedule, site availability, weather and the ability of your dog.

■ **Beginning Training - Contamination and Starts**
■ **Exercise 01**

Exercise	01 - Contamination and Starts Short, motivational starts on contaminated vegetated surfaces
Location	Mowed lawn
Type of Location	Park, Campus, School or Church
Surfaces	Grass
Components	06
Lesson Plan	Lay a minimum of four (4) sets of tracks as diagramed. Work the dog on a six to 10 foot leash length. Be prepared to move up the line and help the dog stay on the track.
Comments	Vegetated area.
	Individual Legs should be a minimum of 50 yards in length.
	These are designed to be fun, motivational tracks. Run them in sets of four (4).

Exercise 01 Contamination
Diagram

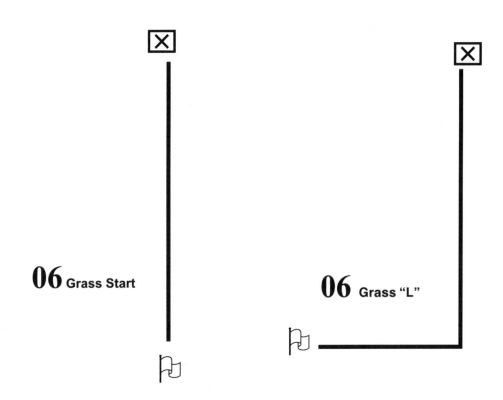

Contaminated Play/Sports Area Such As A School, Campus or Church

TRACKING NOTES

Date: 01/01/00 ☐ AM ✓ PM ✓ Day ☐ Night   Dog: Ace, Border Collie

Location: Eastside Elementary School

Area Description: mowed lawn on and near soccer fields

Tracklayer: Suzie Smith   Handler: Suzie Smith   TL Started: 3:30 pm   Dog Started: 4:30pm

Ground Conditions: low grass, dry   Weather Conditions: cool, breezy   Wind Spd:15mph   Temp 42°

Components Utilized: 06, modified 06

Surfaces: grass   _____   _____   _____   _____

Articles: ✓Fabric ✓Leather ☐ Plastic ☐ Metal

Comments: Good starts. Worked intently on grass. Had problems at first but understood his job and kept working. Call Judy and Heather to see if we can get together Tuesday and Thursday to do some more.

SAMPLE TRAINING MAP
Exercise 01

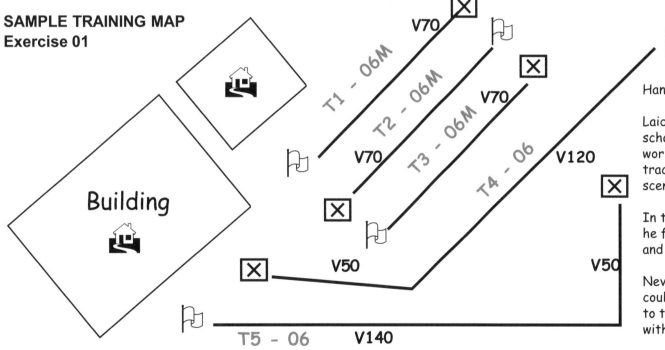

Handler Notes:

Laid tracks about 1 hour after school was let out for the day. He worked very hard on the first few tracks to sort out the hundreds of scents.

In the middle of the fourth track he figured it out and aced the 4th and 5th tracks!

Never would have believed that he could work this hard and stay close to the track on a school ground with all of the cross tracks!

■ **Beginning Training - Contamination, Starts and Transitions**
■ **Exercise 02**

Exercise	**02 - Contamination, Starts and Transitions** Transitions across a road or wide walkway.
Location	Dirt, Sand, Gravel or Mulch Play/Sports Area
Type of Location	Campus, School or Church
Surfaces	Mowed lawn, dirt, stone/gravel or mulch.
Components	01, 06, 07, 08
Lesson Plan	Lay a minimum of four (4) tracks made up of the components listed above as diagramed. Work the dog on a six to 10 foot leash length. When introducing the dog to the transition, be prepared to move up the line and help the dog.
Comments	Vegetated area divided by or near dirt, sand, gravel or mulch play/sports area. Start yardage should be a minimum of 20 yards to transition area or turn. Continue all legs a minimum of 10 yards past transition areas or turns before ending the exercise. Review the section on "Intersecting Stairstep Tracks" (Chapter 16) in *Mastering Variable Surface Tracking: The Component Training Approach*. It may be helpful to utilize a drag to lay additional scent through the contamination for your dog to follow.

Exercise 02 Contamination, Starts and Transitions
Diagram

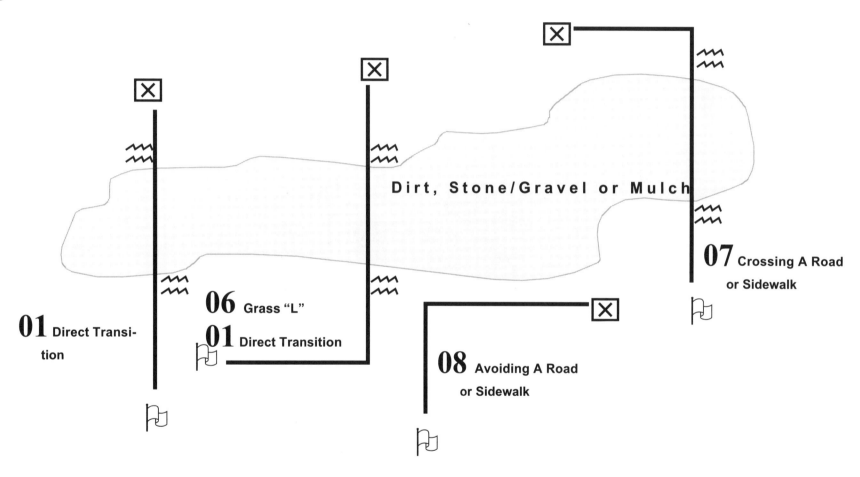

TRACKING NOTES

Date: 1/08/00 ✓ AM ☐ PM ✓ Day ☐ Night   Dog: Ace, Border Collie

Location: City Park - Behind Pavilion in dirt playground area.

Area Description: some mowed lawn, scrub grass, dirt and sand play area

Tracklayer: Bob Smith   Handler: Suzie Smith   TL Started: 7:30am   Dog Started: 8:35am

Ground Conditions: low grass, dirt, damp   Weather Conditions: drizzle, cold   Wind Spd: 5mph   Temp: 37°

Components Utilized: 01, 06, 07, 08

Surfaces: grass   dirt   _____   _____   _____

Articles: ✓Fabric   ✓Leather   ☐   Plastic   ☐   Metal

Comments: Had problems with the first transition into dirt. He searched and searched and finally found one footstep. It was like watching a light bulb turn on. He searched for the next, and then the next and soon, he was actually tracking. The second track was much easier for him. This is going to be a lot of fun!

SAMPLE TRAINING MAP
Exercise 02

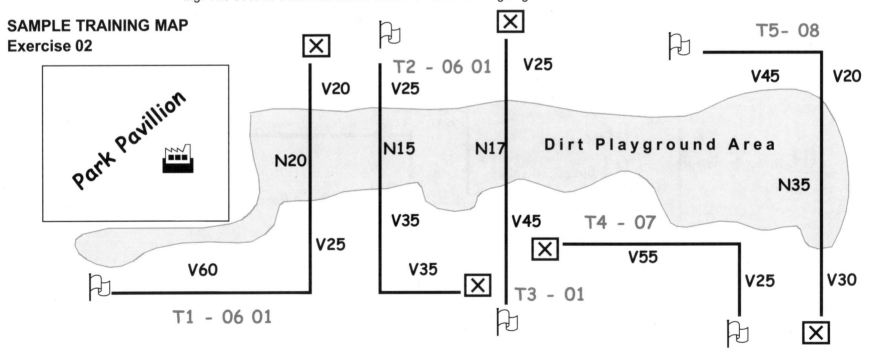

8

- **Beginning Training - Starts and Transitions**
- **Exercise 03**

Exercise	**03 - Contamination, Starts and Transitions** Transitions across of a road or wide walkway.
Location	An asphalt, concrete, dirt or gravel road surrounded by mowed lawns or fields.
Type of Location	Business/Industrial Park, Campus, School or Church
Surfaces	Mowed lawn, asphalt, cement, dirt, stone/gravel or mulch
Components	01, 06, 07, 08
Lesson Plan	Lay a minimum of four (4) tracks made up of the components listed above as diagramed. Work the dog on a six to 10 foot leash length. When introducing the dog to the transition, be prepared to move up the line and help the dog.
Comments	Non-vegetated roads or wide walkways without curbs or gutters.
	Start yardage should be a minimum of 20 yards to transition area or turn. Continue all legs a minimum of 10 yards past transition areas or turns before ending the exercise.
	Review the section on "Transition Components" (Chapter 17) of *Mastering Variable Surface Tracking: The Component Training Approach.* Utilize handprints or drags (page 116) to assist your dog in working across and not "jumping" the non-vegetated area.

Exercise 03 Starts and Transitions
Diagram

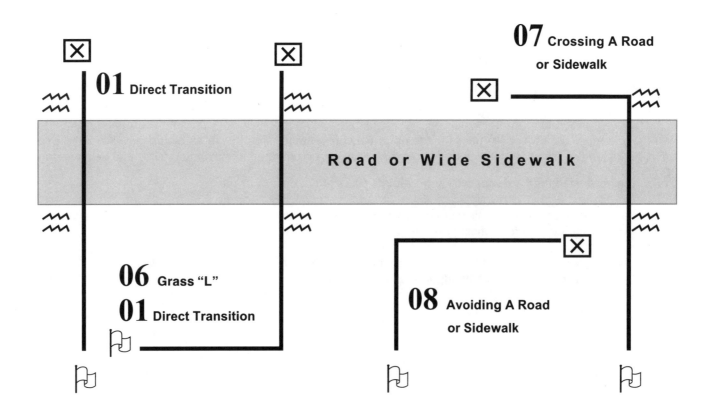

TRACKING NOTES

Date: 1/15/00 ✓ AM ☐ PM ✓ Day ☐ Night   Dog: Ace, Border Collie
Location: Northwest Industrial Park - Acme Manufacturing Company
Area Description: mowed lawn with 3 lane asphalt drive (about 18 yards wide), no curbs/gutters
Tracklayer: Suzie Smith   Handler: Suzie Smith   TL Started: 8:15am   Dog Started: 9:55am
Ground Conditions: low grass, dry   Weather Conditions: cool, damp   Wind Spd: 0mph   Temp: 49°
Components Utilized: 01, 06, 07, 08
Surfaces: grass   asphalt   _____   _____   _____   _____
Articles: ✓Fabric ✓Leather   ☐ Plastic ☐ Metal
Comments: Good starts. Worked intently on grass. Hesitating to work on asphalt. Wanted to jump road. After 4 tracks he started to venture on road looking for track. Try drags or handprints next outing to help him accept asphalt surface.

SAMPLE TRAINING MAP
Exercise 03

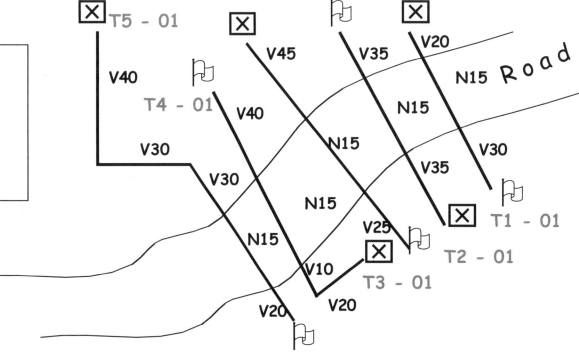

■ **Beginning Training - Starts Involving Sidewalks**
■ **Exercise 04**

Exercise	04 - Starts Involving Sidewalks
	Incorporating sidewalks into starts.
Location	Grass area with non-vegetated sidewalk or walkway or road with parallel sidewalk.
Type of Location	Business/Industrial Park, Campus, School or Church, Office Building
Surfaces	Mowed lawn
Components	07, 08
Lesson Plan	Lay a minimum of four (4) tracks made up of the components listed above as diagramed. Work the dog on a six to 10 foot leash length. When introducing the dog to the transition, be prepared to move up the line and help the dog.
Comments	Vegetated area divided by sidewalk and/or road with parallel sidewalk

Start yardage should be a minimum of 20 yards to transition area or turn. Continue all legs a minimum of 10 yards past transition areas or turns before ending the exercise.

Sidewalks are typically lower than surrounding grasses, therefore scent will tend to collect at the edges of the vegetated area. Many dogs will fringe this area. In situations where sidewalks are surrounded by porous non-vegetated surfaces such as loose dirt, sand, stones, or gravel, the scent will collect along the edge of the sidewalk. When sidewalks are surrounded by asphalt, cement, or concrete type surfaces, the scent may tend to flow from the sidewalk along any grade on the surrounding surface.

Exercise 04 Starts Involving Sidewalks
Diagram

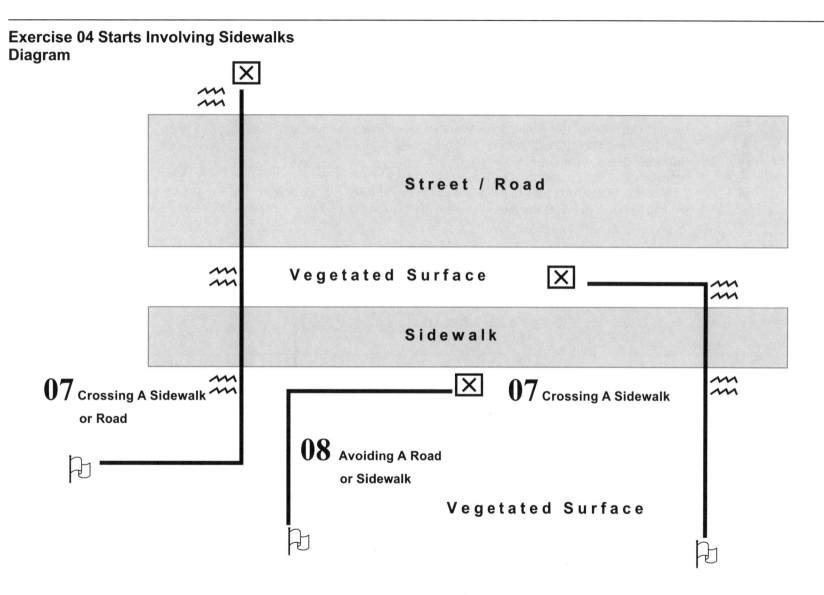

TRACKING NOTES

Date: 1/22/00 ✓ AM ☐ PM ✓ Day ☐ Night   Dog: Ace, Border Collie
Location: City street
Area Description: city street with sidewalk in front of administration building
Tracklayer: Heather Jones   Handler: Suzie Smith   TL Started: 7:40am   Dog Started: 8:25am
Ground Conditions: low grass, dry   Weather Conditions: clear, cold   Wind Spd: 12mph   Temp: 35°
Components Utilized: 01, 07, 08
Surfaces: grass   cement   _____   _____   _____   _____
Articles: ✓Fabric ✓Leather   ☐   Plastic   ☐   Metal
Comments: Initially dog tried to jump sidewalk when turning before sidewalk. Shortened up on line (to 6 feet) and worked with him to locate the turn. Also tried to jump road but quickly understood that track was not on other side.

SAMPLE TRAINING MAP
Exercise 04

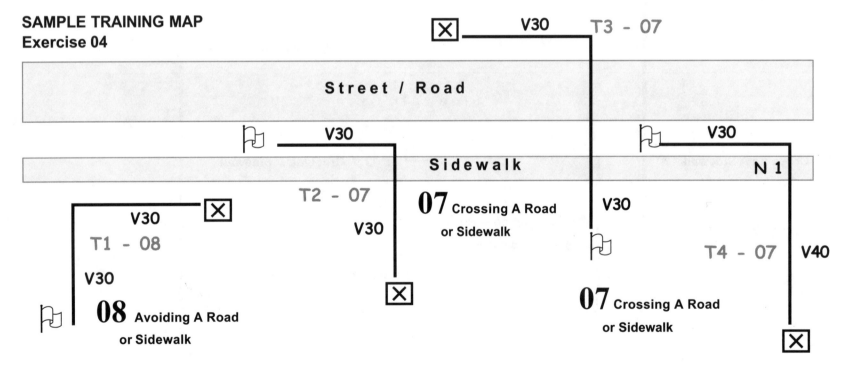

■ Beginning Training - Starts Involving Hedges/Fences
■ Exercise 05

Exercise	05 - Starts Involving Hedges/Fences Incorporating hedges and fences starts.
Location	Grass area with hedges and/or fences.
Type of Location	Business/Industrial Park, Campus, School or Church, Office Building
Surfaces	Mowed lawn, mulch, gravel/stone
Components	41, 42, 43, 44, 45, 46
Lesson Plan	Lay a minimum of four (4) tracks made up of the components listed above as diagramed. Work the dog on a six to 10 foot leash length. When introducing the dog to the transition, be prepared to move up the line and help the dog.
Comments	Start yardage should be a minimum of 20 yards to transition area or turn. Continue all legs a minimum of 10 yards past transition areas or turns before ending the exercise. Review the section on "Fences, Hedges and Walls" (Chapter 21) of ***Mastering Variable Surface Tracking: The Componenet Training Approach*** for information on the effect various types of fence material and construction may have on the scent from a track in their vicinity.

Exercise 05 Starts Involving Hedges/Fences
Diagram

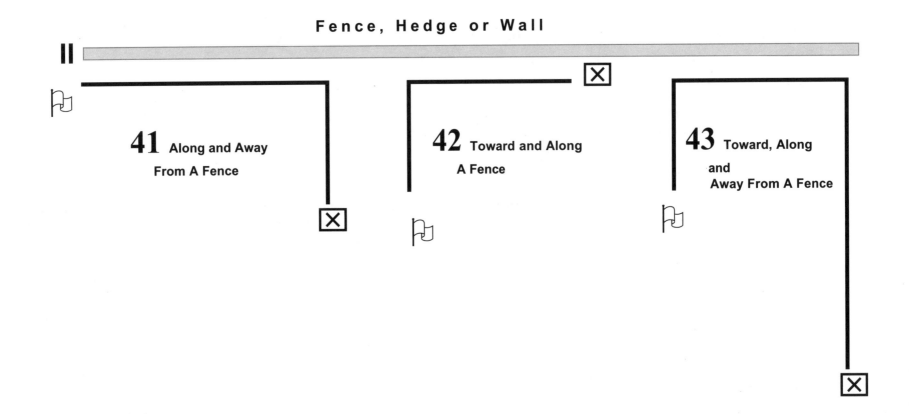

Exercise 05 Starts Involving Hedges/Fences
Diagram

Fence, Hedge or Wall

44 Parallel To and
Between A Fence

45 Between A Fence

46 Open Turn Away
From A Fence

Exercise 05 Starts Involving Hedges/Fences
Diagram

Chain Link Fence

Plastic Snow Fence

Wood Fence

Stone or Brick Fence

Vegetated Hedges

Work each of the proceeding five (5) components utilizing all of the above types of fences and hedges you may find in your training area or that you might expect to find in a test location. Expect these surfaces to pull the dog into the fence as the surface will collect scent. You will notice that the various surfaces of the fence material hold scent in different ways. The stone and wood surfaces will tend to collect scent along the bottom edge of the material while plastic and chain link collect scent along the entire mesh surface. Vegetated hedges tend to pool scent between the plants and the dog may want to work between the hedges even when the track parallels the hedge.

TRACKING NOTES

Date: 1/29/00 ✓ AM ☐ PM ✓ Day ☐ Night   Dog: Ace, Border Collie
Location: Northwest Industrial Park - Acme Manufacturing Company
Area Description: mowed lawn with hedges, fences and walls
Tracklayer: Suzie Smith   Handler: Suzie Smith   TL Started: 9:15am   Dog Started: 10:55am

Ground Conditions: low grass, damp   Weather Conditions: cool, damp   Wind Spd: 10mph   Temp: 70⁰
Components Utilized: 41, 42, 43, 44, 45, 46
Surfaces: grass _____ _____ _____ _____
Articles: ✓Fabric ✓Leather ☐ Plastic ☐ Metal
Comments: Wind collected scent on crosswind legs and pulled dog into the fences. Need to bring Heather here to show her how Ace reacts to hedges and buildings.

SAMPLE TRAINING MAP
Exercise 05

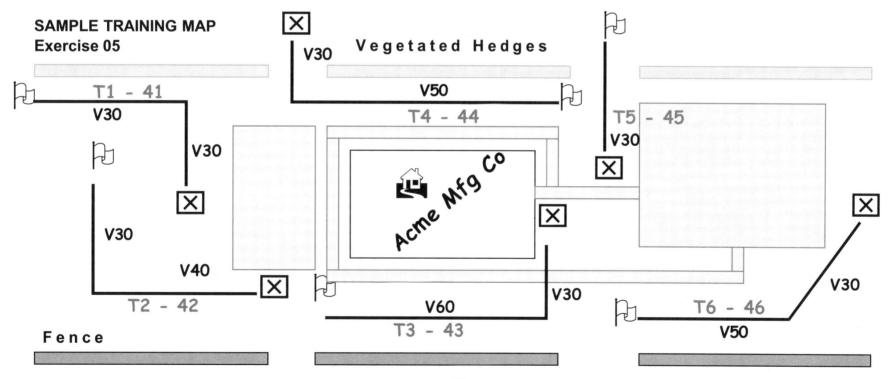

■ **Beginning Training** - **Starts Involving Buildings**
■ **Exercise 06**

Exercise	06 - Starts Involving Buildings Incorporating buildings into starts.
Location	Grass area with buildings
Type of Location	Business/Industrial Park, Campus, School or Office Building
Surfaces	Mowed lawn, cement, gravel, mulch
Components	35, 36, 37, 38, 39, 40
Lesson Plan	Lay a minimum of four (4) tracks made up of the components listed above as diagramed. Work the dog on a six to 10 foot leash length. When introducing the dog to the transition, be prepared to move up the line and help the dog.
Comments	Start yardage should be a minimum of 20 yards to transition area or turn. Continue all legs a minimum of 10 yards past transition areas or turns before ending the exercise.
	Review the section on "Building Components" (Chapter 20) of *Mastering Variable Surface Tracking: The Component Training Approach* for additional information on Building Shadow and wind effect for one or more buildings.

Exercise 06 Starts Involving Buildings
Diagram

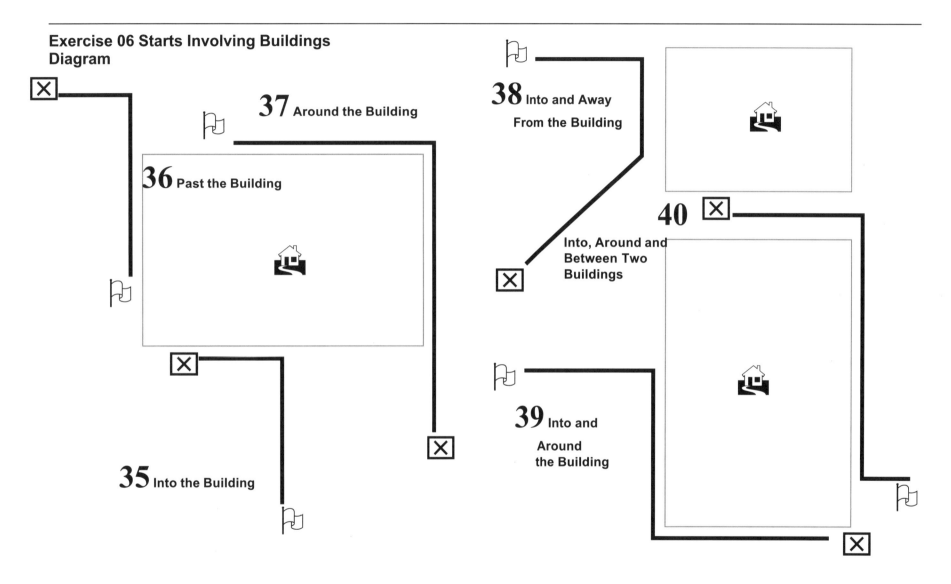

37 Around the Building

38 Into and Away From the Building

36 Past the Building

40 Into, Around and Between Two Buildings

35 Into the Building

39 Into and Around the Building

TRACKING NOTES

Date: 2/05/00 ☐ AM ✓ PM ✓ Day ☐ Night   Dog: Ace, Border Collie
Location: City College
Area Description: mowed lawn with building(s)
Tracklayer: Suzie Smith   Handler: Suzie Smith   TL Started: 1:20pm   Dog Started: 2:46pm
Ground Conditions: low grass, heavy dew   Weather Conditions: light fog   Wind Spd: 0mph   Temp: 63°
Components Utilized: 35, 36, 37
Surfaces: grass   cement   _____   _____   _____
Articles: ✓Fabric ✓Leather ☐ Plastic ☐ Metal
Comments: It was easy to see footsteps and tell when he was on track.

SAMPLE TRAINING MAP
Exercise 06

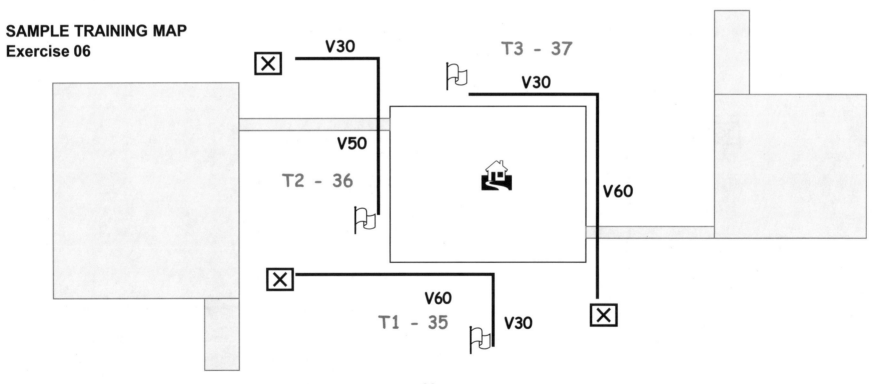

TRACKING NOTES

Date: 2/12/00 ✓ AM ☐ PM ✓ Day ☐ Night   Dog: Ace, Border Collie
Location: City College
Area Description: mowed lawn with building(s)
Tracklayer: Judy Collins   Handler: Suzie Smith   TL Started: 6:45am   Dog Started: 8:38am
Ground Conditions: low grass, damp   Weather Conditions: damp, cool   Wind Spd: 5mph   Temp: 52°
Components Utilized: 38, 39, 40
Surfaces: grass   cement   gravel   _____   _____
Articles: ✓Fabric ✓Leather ☐ Plastic ☐ Metal
Comments: Ace worked a lot closer to the building than I expected. Even with such a light wind, he was consistently drawn off track 2-3 yards to the building edge. Had some difficulty with the swirling wind between buildings.

SAMPLE TRAINING MAP
Exercise 06

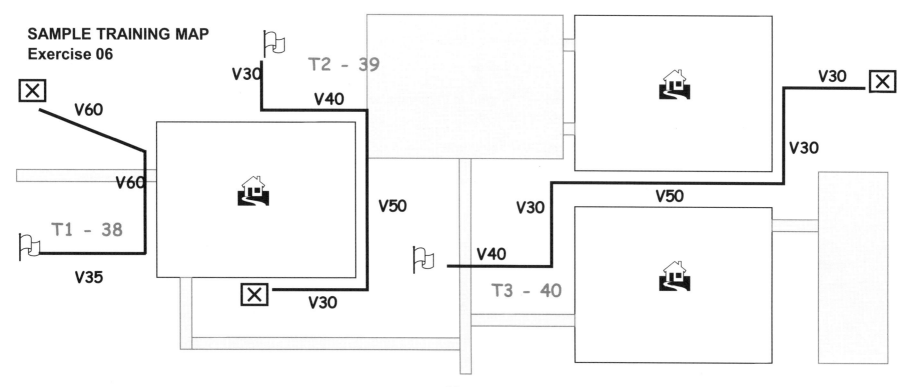

■ **Beginning Training - Starts Involving Berms/Islands/Esplanades**
■ **Exercise 07**

Exercise	07 - Starts Involving Berms/Islands/Esplanades Incorporating berms, islands and esplanades into starts.
Location	Grass area with berms. Streets with esplanades, parking lots with islands.
Type of Location	Business/Industrial Park, Campus, School or Church, Office Building, City Street
Surfaces	Mowed lawn, concrete, asphalt
Components	13, 25, 28, 29, 31, 33, 34,
Lesson Plan	Lay a minimum of four (4) tracks made up of the components listed above as diagramed. Work the dog on a six to 10 foot leash length. When introducing the dog to the transition, be prepared to move up the line and help the dog.
Comments	Parking lots with islands, and/or streets with esplanades.

Start yardage should be a minimum of 20 yards to transition area or turn. Continue all legs a minimum of 10 yards past transition areas or turns before ending the exercise.

When tracking on or across berms, watch for subtle indications that your dog is following scent that is being pushed down the grade. When working islands or esplanades, watch for indications from your dog of the scent drifting along the curb of the island. Your dog may work partially or completely around an island before determining the track location and direction. Always be alert for moving traffic in these areas; and expect to find some or all of your articles left in this area either moved or missing.

Exercise 07 Starts Involving Berms/Islands/Esplanades
Diagram

13 Start on an Island
or Esplanade

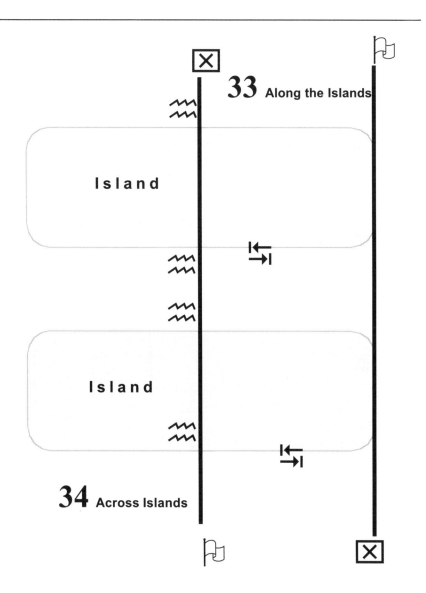

33 Along the Islands

34 Across Islands

Exercise 07 Starts Involving Berms/Islands/Esplanades
Diagram

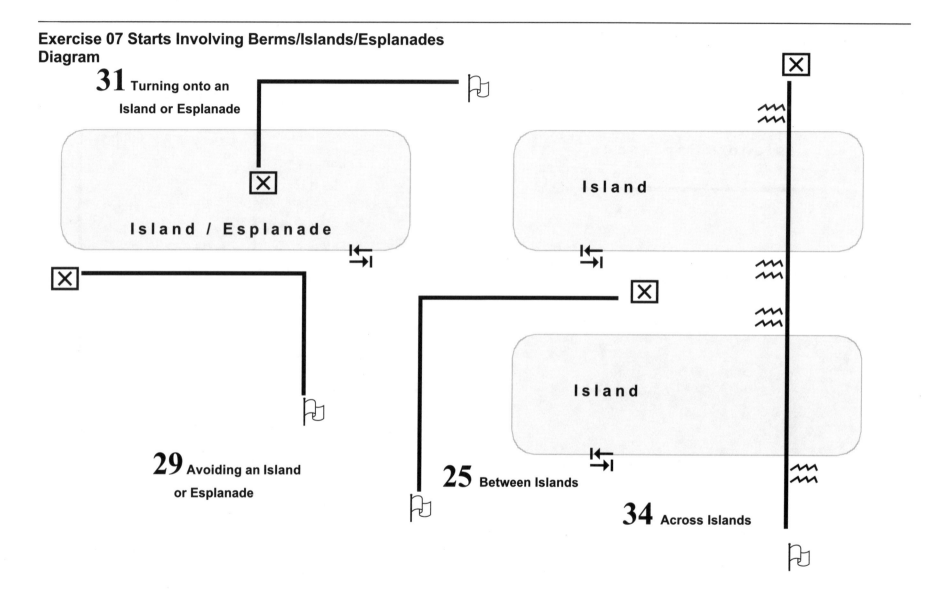

31 Turning onto an Island or Esplanade

Island / Esplanade

Island

Island

29 Avoiding an Island or Esplanade

25 Between Islands

34 Across Islands

Exercise 07 Starts Involving Berms/Islands/Esplanades Diagram

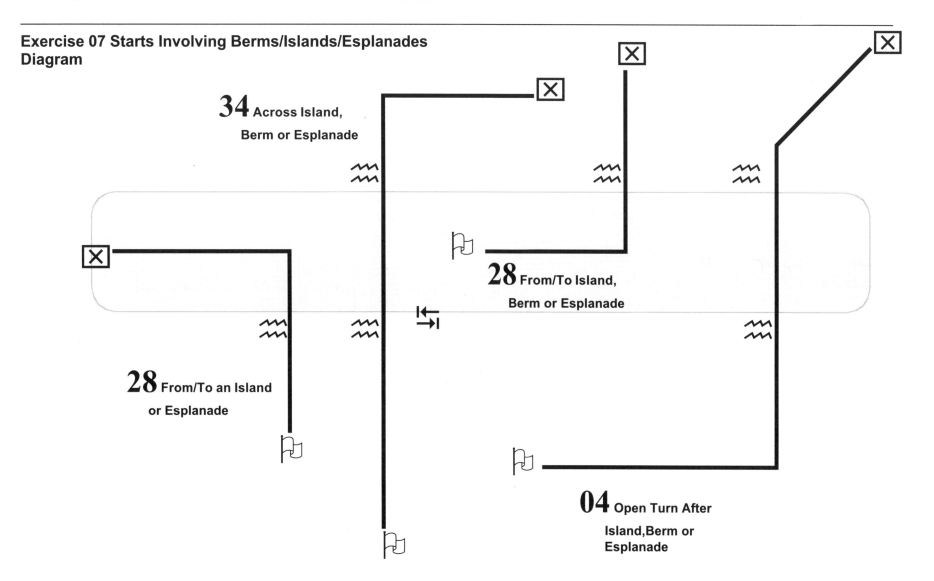

34 Across Island, Berm or Esplanade

28 From/To Island, Berm or Esplanade

28 From/To an Island or Esplanade

04 Open Turn After Island, Berm or Esplanade

TRACKING NOTES

Date: 2/19/00 ✓ AM ☐ PM ✓ Day ☐ Night   Dog: Ace, Border Collie
Location: RPM Technologies employee parking area
Area Description: parking lot with islands
Tracklayer: Heather Jones   Handler: Suzie Smith   TL Started: 7:18am   Dog Started: 8:52am
Ground Conditions: dry   Weather Conditions: clear, dry   Wind Spd: 10mph   Temp: 50°
Components Utilized: 13, 28, 33, 34
Surfaces: grass   asphalt   mulch _____   _____
Articles: ✓Fabric ✓Leather   ☐   Plastic ☐ Metal
Comments: Worked intently along curb surrounding islands; crossing grass and ground cover was much easier for him than working the mulch or dirt areas. We will need to repeat this exercise often to get better!

SAMPLE TRAINING MAP
Exercise 07

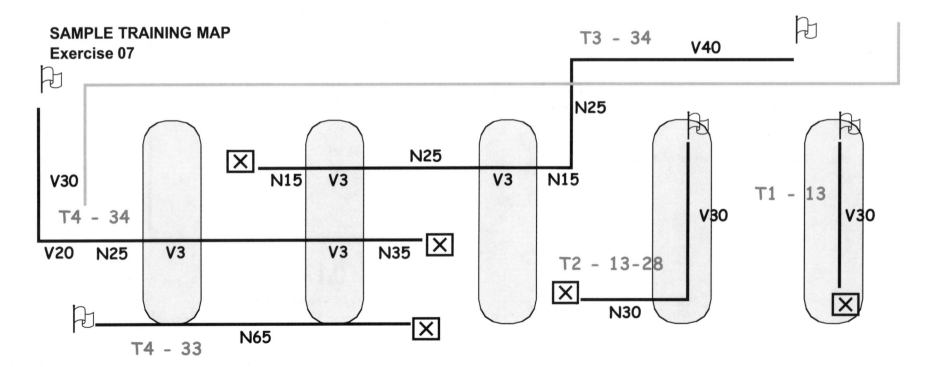

TRACKING NOTES

Date: 2/26/00 ✓ AM ☐ PM ✓ Day ☐ Night   Dog: Ace, Border Collie
Location: RPM Technologies employee parking area
Area Description: parking lot with islands
Tracklayer: Suzie Smith   Handler: Suzie Smith   TL Started: 8:45am   Dog Started: 9:40am
Ground Conditions: dry   Weather Conditions: clear   Wind Spd: 5mph   Temp: 550°
Components Utilized: 13, 28, 33, 34
Surfaces: grass   asphalt   mulch   _____   _____   _____
Articles: ✓Fabric ✓Leather ☐ Plastic ☐ Metal
Comments: Ace worked much better today and is becoming more comfortable transitioning to and from the islands.
He is still searching the curb areas but has started to keep his nose down on mulch and dirt surfaces. More Work!!

SAMPLE TRAINING MAP
Exercise 07

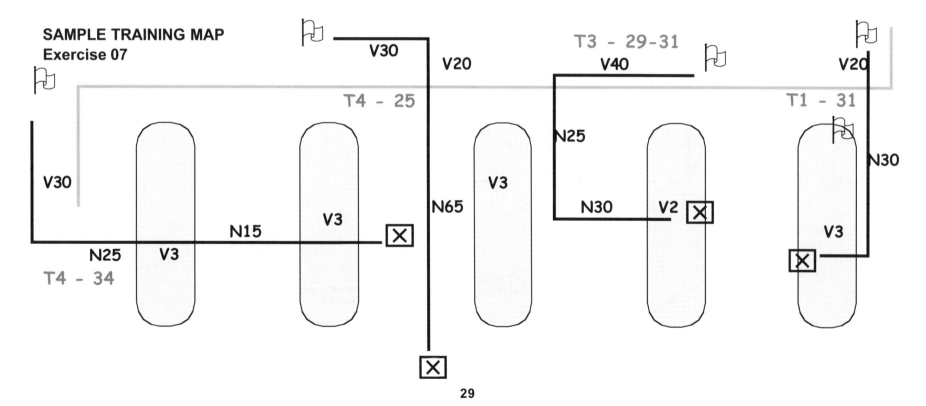

TRACKING NOTES

Date: 3/04/00 ☐ AM ✓ PM ✓ Day ☐ Night   Dog: Ace, Border Collie
Location: RPM Technologies employee parking area
Area Description: parking lot with islands
Tracklayer: Bob Smith   Handler: Suzie Smith   TL Started: 2:30pm   Dog Started: 4:50pm
Ground Conditions: low grass, dry   Weather Conditions: warm   Wind Spd: 0mph   Temp: 69°
Components Utilized: 01, 06, 07, 08
Surfaces: grass   asphalt   mulch   _____   _____   _____
Articles: ✓Fabric ✓Leather ☐ Plastic ☐ Metal
Comments: Starting to progress nicely, our intermediate work of this exercise has really helped us. Ace now searches briefly at the curb edge before determining the track has continued onto/off the island. We're getting better!

SAMPLE TRAINING MAP
Exercise 07

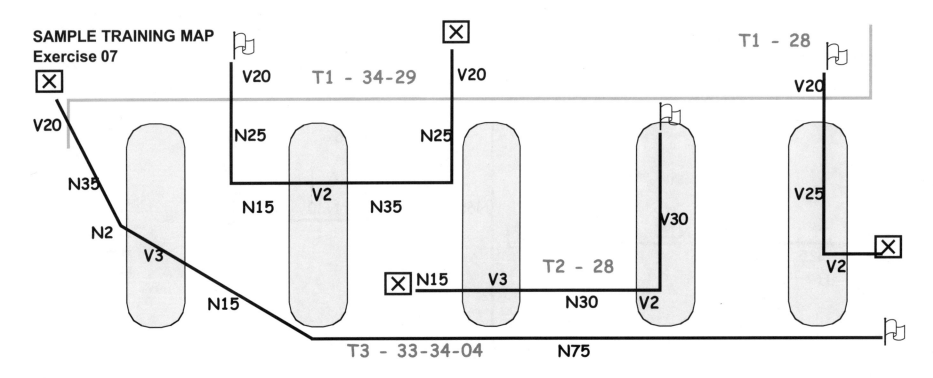

■ Beginning Training **- Starts Involving Lakes/Ponds**
■ **Exercise 08**

Exercise	08 - Starts Involving Lakes/Ponds
	Starts near lakes or ponds
Location	Vegetated areas near a lake or pond.
Type of Location	Business/Industrial Park, Campus, School or Church, Office Building
Surfaces	Mowed lawn
Components	15, 16
Lesson Plan	Lay a minimum of four (4) tracks made up of the components listed above as diagramed. Work the dog on a six to 10 foot leash length. When introducing the dog to the transition, be prepared to move up the line and help the dog.
Comments	Start yardage should be a minimum of 20 yards to transition area or turn. Continue all legs a minimum of 10 yards past transition areas or turns before ending the exercise.
	Tracks laid near lakes and ponds, the scent will be drawn toward the water and will spread out along the surface and collect along the edges. As your dog follows the track, he may be drawn to the water's edge and give you his indication for loss of track. Allow your dog to search these areas, while watching him for his indications. Encourage your dog to remain near the track. In many such locations, you will find waterfowl and other types of wildlife which may distract your dog from tracking.

Exercise 08 Starts Involving Lakes/Ponds
Diagram

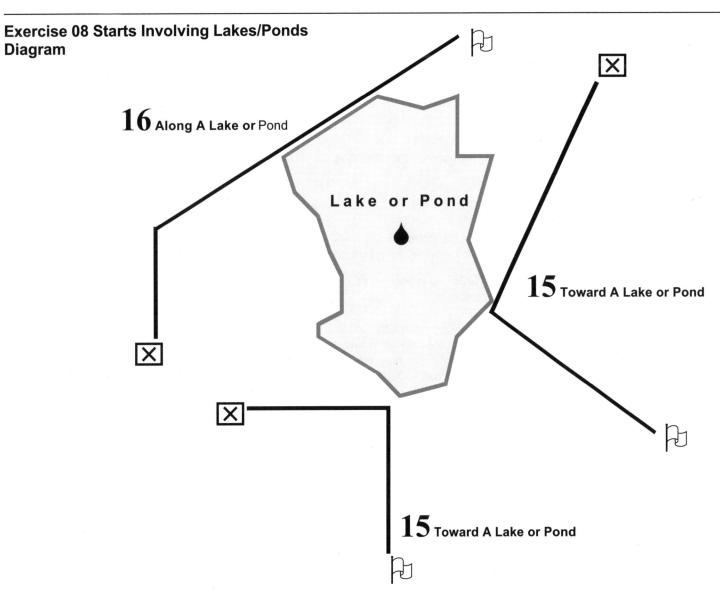

16 Along A Lake or Pond

Lake or Pond

15 Toward A Lake or Pond

15 Toward A Lake or Pond

TRACKING NOTES

Date: 3/11/00   ☐ AM ✓ PM ✓ Day ☐ Night   Dog: Ace, Border Collie
Location: Citywest Office Park
Area Description: grassy area around duck ponds
Tracklayer: Bob Smith   Handler: Suzie Smith   TL Started: 4:00pm   Dog Started: 5:15pm
Ground Conditions: low grass, damp   Weather Conditions: light rain   Wind Spd: 5mph   Temp: 60°
Components Utilized: 01, 06, 07, 08
Surfaces: grass   grass   dirt   sand   _____   _____
Articles: ✓Fabric   ✓Leather   ☐   Plastic   ☐   Metal
Comments: Ace tried to herd all the ducks on the first two tracks, but I finally got him to work. This exercise is going to need to be repeated often to get him used to working around animals.

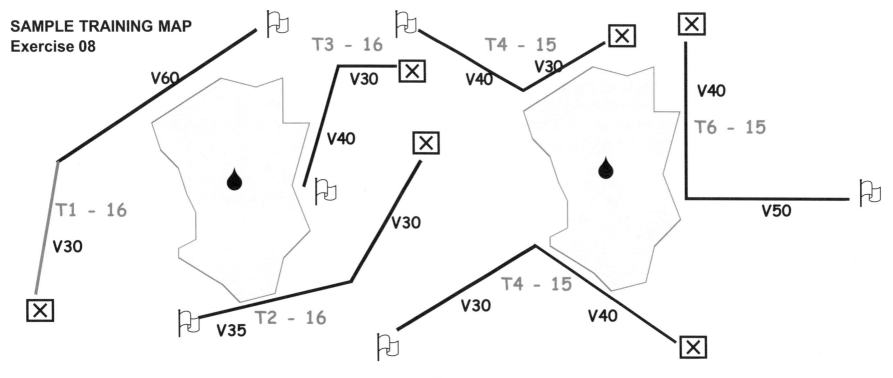

SAMPLE TRAINING MAP
Exercise 08

Advanced Training

At this point in your training you and your dog should be confident in working in varied urban locations. The initial lesson plans you have completed are the foundation which you will now start to build on to create a working team. Linking together components using start components and transition components allows you to develop an almost unlimited number of tracking possibilities for your training location. As you continue in your training, you will start to link together more and more components until you are able to easily develop test length training tracks.

Remember that at any time you can go back to an earlier chapter to work on a single component, routine or training session should you or your dog start to regress in training. Variable surface tracking is a strenuous activity for both you and your dog. It may, at times, appear to be much more mentally tiring than physically challenging. Continue to train using the components as laid out in the lesson plans. The natural tendency is to jump ahead and start to lay full length tracks. However, without introducing your dog to the scenting problems developed in many of the following lessons, he will not develop the problem solving and work ethics required to avoid the multitude of distractions in an urban environment while working his track. More importantly, as a team member, you may start to miss the subtle indications he gives you as he works the track.

By linking together various start and transition components which fit into your training area together with the new component you will be working on you should start to see a marked improvement in your dog's ability to stay on track.

■ Advanced Training - **Combining Starts and Transitions**
■ **Exercise 09**

Exercise	09 - Combining Starts and Transitions.
Location	Vegetated area incorporating multiple transitions
Type of Location	Business/Industrial Park, Campus, School or Church, Office Building
Surfaces	Multiple
Components	As selected
Lesson Plan	Lay the components selected as diagramed. Continue to work the components in this exercise until your dog is confident working these scenting and surface transition problems and you are becoming comfortable with reading your dog's track indications.
Comments	Start yardage should be a minimum of 20 yards to transition area or turn. Continue all legs a minimum of 10 yards past transition areas or turns before ending the exercise.

Exercise 9 Combining Starts and Transitions Diagram

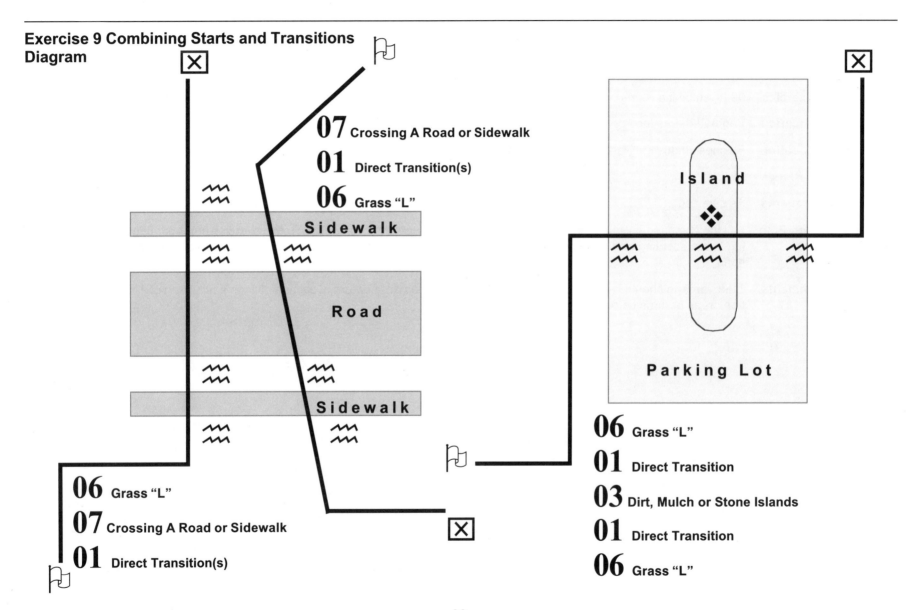

07 Crossing A Road or Sidewalk

01 Direct Transition(s)

06 Grass "L"

S i d e w a l k

R o a d

S i d e w a l k

06 Grass "L"

07 Crossing A Road or Sidewalk

01 Direct Transition(s)

I s l a n d

P a r k i n g   L o t

06 Grass "L"

01 Direct Transition

03 Dirt, Mulch or Stone Islands

01 Direct Transition

06 Grass "L"

Exercise 9 Combining Starts and Transitions
Diagram

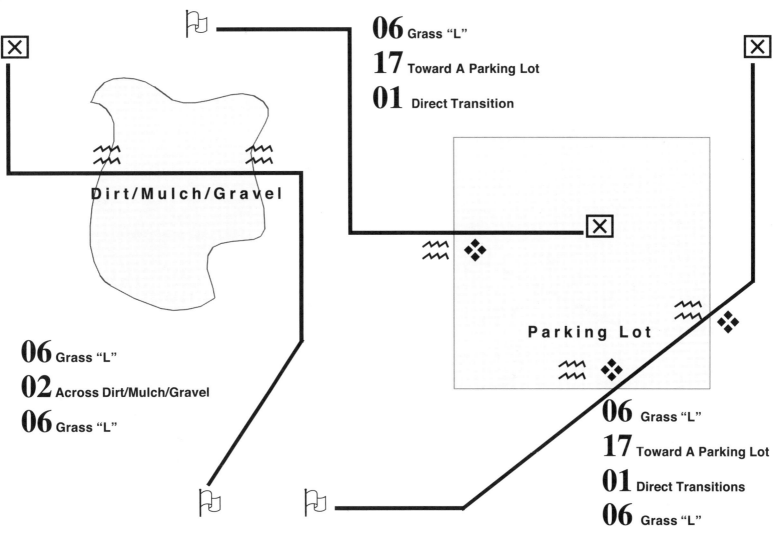

06 Grass "L"

17 Toward A Parking Lot

01 Direct Transition

Dirt/Mulch/Gravel

06 Grass "L"

02 Across Dirt/Mulch/Gravel

06 Grass "L"

Parking Lot

06 Grass "L"

17 Toward A Parking Lot

01 Direct Transitions

06 Grass "L"

Exercise 9 Combining Starts and Transitions
Diagram

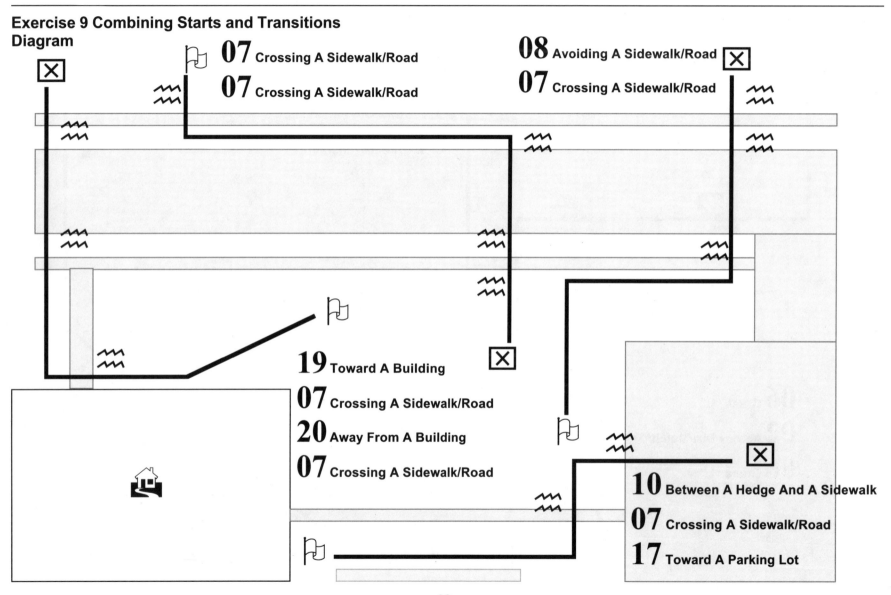

07 Crossing A Sidewalk/Road

07 Crossing A Sidewalk/Road

08 Avoiding A Sidewalk/Road

07 Crossing A Sidewalk/Road

19 Toward A Building

07 Crossing A Sidewalk/Road

20 Away From A Building

07 Crossing A Sidewalk/Road

10 Between A Hedge And A Sidewalk

07 Crossing A Sidewalk/Road

17 Toward A Parking Lot

TRACKING NOTES

Date: 3/18/00 ☐ AM ✓ PM ✓ Day ☐ Night   Dog: Ace, Border Collie

Location: Smithfield Campus - Parking Lot "B"

Area Description: campus parking lot and access road with sidewalks

Tracklayer: Heather Jones   Handler: Suzie Smith   TL Started: 3:30pm   Dog Started: 5:40pm

Ground Conditions: low grass, dry   Weather Conditions: clear   Wind Spd: 3mph   Temp: 63°

Components Utilized: 01, 03, 06, 07

Surfaces: grass   asphalt   cement   _____   _____   _____

Articles: ✓Fabric   ✓Leather   ☐ Plastic   ☐ Metal

Comments: After working as intently as we did on the islands, I feel that Ace handled these components easily. The people around the campus distracted him and we'll have to repeat this exercise multiple times.

SAMPLE TRAINING MAP
Exercise 09

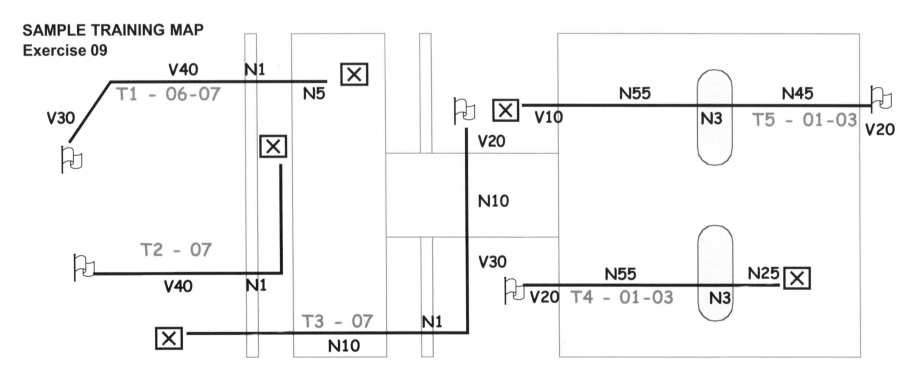

TRACKING NOTES

Date: 3/25/00 ✓ AM ☐ PM ✓ Day ☐ Night   Dog: Ace, Border Collie
Location: Smithfield Campus - Parking Lot "F" and playground area
Area Description: Parking lot near playground
Tracklayer: Judy Collins   Handler: Suzie Smith   TL Started: 6:18am   Dog Started: 9:20am
Ground Conditions: damp   Weather Conditions: cool, drizzle   Wind Spd: 10mph   Temp: 55°
Components Utilized: 07
Surfaces: grass   asphalt   dirt   sand   _____   _____
Articles: ✓Fabric ✓Leather ☐ Plastic ☐ Metal
Comments: Damp sand appeared quite easy for Ace to work on. Footsteps were visible, so it was easy to know he was on track. Damp asphalt made it seem easier for him to stay closer to the track. Try this again under different weather (wet, dry, sunny, cloudy) to see if it makes a difference.

SAMPLE TRAINING MAP
Exercise 09

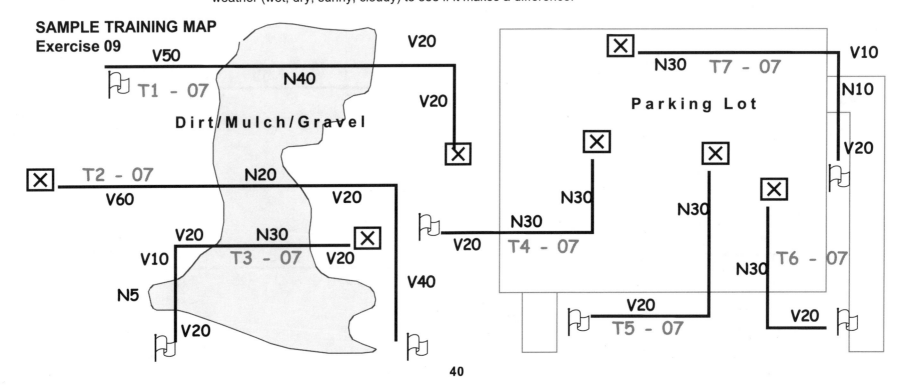

TRACKING NOTES

Date: 4/01/00 ✓ AM ☐ PM ✓ Day ☐ Night   Dog: Ace, Border Collie
Location: City Library complex
Area Description: Parking lots near buildings
Tracklayer: Suzie Smith   Handler: Suzie Smith   TL Started: 6:35am   Dog Started: 10:15am
Ground Conditions: wet, slick   Weather Conditions: light rain, sleet   Wind Spd: 20mph   Temp: 31°
Components Utilized: 06, 07, 17, 23, 37
Surfaces: grass   asphalt   concrete   _____   _____   _____
Articles: ✓Fabric ✓Leather   ☐   Plastic ☐   Metal
Comments: Cold, miserable working conditions. It was cold and dry when I laid it, the change in weather really affected the scenting conditions. He worked and worked, but in some places the track just "disappeared." Work this several more time in "better" conditions! Hope there's no test in these conditions.

SAMPLE TRAINING MAP

Exercise 09

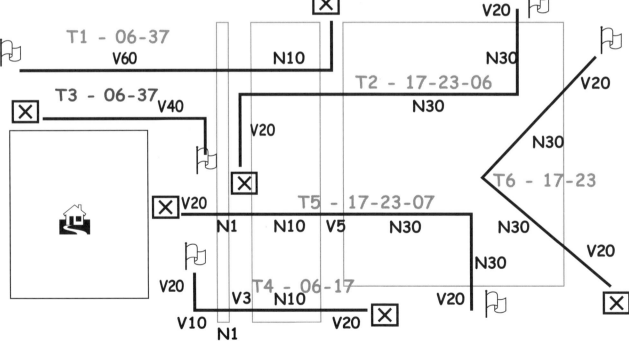

■ **Advanced Training - Incorporating Turn Components**
■ **Exercise 10**

Exercise	10 - incorporating Turn Components
Location	Vegetated area incorporating multiple transitions
Type of Location	Business/Industrial Park, Campus, School or Church, Office Building
Surfaces	Multiple
Components	as selected

Lesson Plan Lay the components selected as diagramed. Continue to work the components in this exercise until your dog is confident working these scenting and surface transition problems and you are becoming comfortable with reading your dog's track indications.

Comments Start yardage should be a minimum of 20 yards to transition area or turn. Continue all legs a minimum of 10 yards past transition areas or turns before ending the exercise.

Turns will be on various surfaces as dictated by the terrain. Working through the various components as displayed will prepare your team to meet the challenges of test day.

Exercise 10 Incorporating Turn Components
Diagram

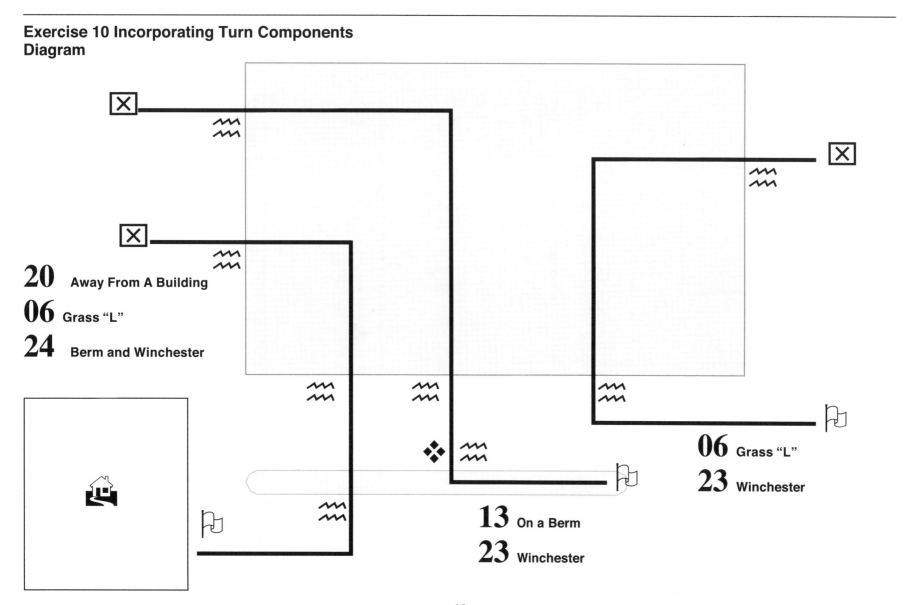

20 Away From A Building

06 Grass "L"

24 Berm and Winchester

06 Grass "L"

23 Winchester

13 On a Berm

23 Winchester

Exercise 10 Incorporating Turn Components Diagram

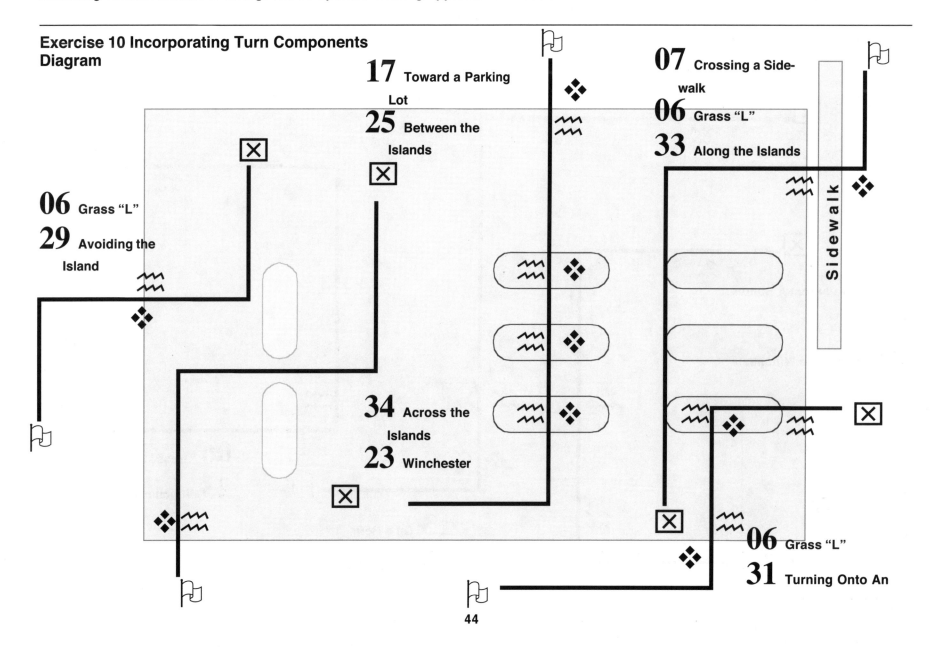

17 Toward a Parking Lot

25 Between the Islands

07 Crossing a Side-walk

06 Grass "L"

33 Along the Islands

06 Grass "L"

29 Avoiding the Island

Sidewalk

34 Across the Islands

23 Winchester

06 Grass "L"

31 Turning Onto An

TRACKING NOTES

Date: 4/08/00 ✓ AM ☐ PM ✓ Day ☐ Night   Dog: Ace, Border Collie
Location: Northwest Industrial Park - SeaBay Engineering PL #2
Area Description: Smithfield Campus - Parking Lot "D"
Tracklayer: Judy Collins   Handler: Suzie Smith   TL Started: 7:15am   Dog Started: 10:05am

Ground Conditions: damp   Weather Conditions: damp, cool   Wind Spd: 10mph   Temp: 55°
Components Utilized: 06, 17, 23, 24, 28, 34
Surfaces: grass   asphalt   gravel   _____   _____   _____
Articles: ✓Fabric ✓Leather ☐ Plastic ☐ Metal
Comments: Much nicer than last Saturday!! Judy used a drag on the first two corners, which really seemed to motivate Ace to stay directly on the track. His head appears to be much higher when working on the asphalt; this tracking style will take some getting used to.

SAMPLE TRAINING MAP
Exercise 10

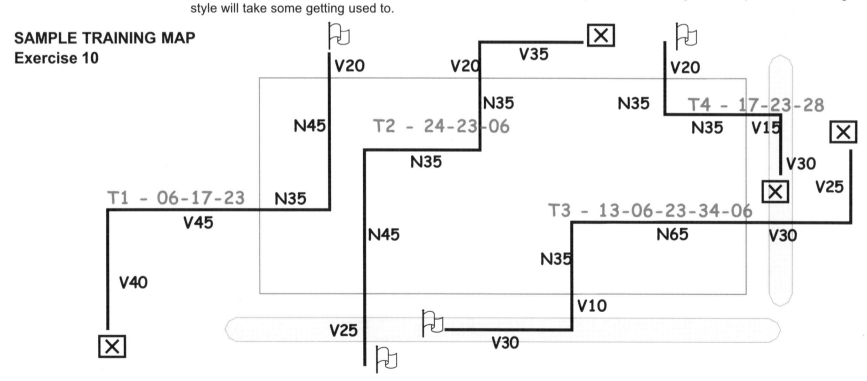

TRACKING NOTES

Date: 4/15/00 ✓ AM ☐ PM ✓ Day ☐ Night   Dog: Ace, Border Collie
Location: Northwest Industrial Park - SeaBay Engineering
Area Description: parking lot with islands and berms
Tracklayer: Heather Jones   Handler: Suzie Smith   TL Started: 6:21am   Dog Started:9:45am
Ground Conditions: low grass, dry   Weather Conditions: dry, windy   Wind Spd: 25mph   Temp: 67°
Components Utilized: 06, 13, 17, 23, 24, 25, 29, 34
Surfaces: grass   asphalt   cement   _____   _____   _____
Articles: ✓Fabric ✓Leather ✓Plastic ☐ Metal
Comments: T1 - crossed berm no problem, entered PL, worked on instead of next to islands. Very proud he corrected himself and went back to track without help. T2 - walked past plastic article at end without indication. Call Judy about playing Article Game (again!) this week.

SAMPLE TRAINING MAP
Exercise 10

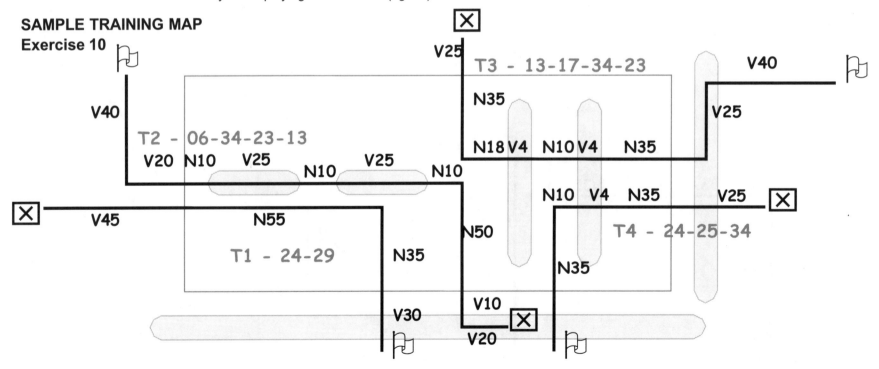

TRACKING NOTES

Date: 4/22/00 ☐ AM ✓ PM ☐ Day ✓ Night   Dog: Ace, Border Collie
Location: Northwest Industrial Park - hotel parking area
Area Description: Parking lot with islands and berms
Tracklayer: Bob Smith   Handler: Suzie Smith   TL Started: 8:15pm   Dog Started: 10:35pm
Ground Conditions: low grass, dry   Weather Conditions: cloudy, warm   Wind Spd: 0mph   Temp: 70°
Components Utilized: 06, 13, 17, 23, 24, 28, 29, 33, 34
Surfaces: grass   asphalt   cement   _____   _____   _____
Articles: ✓Fabric ✓Leather ✓Plastic ✓Metal
Comments: Good starts. Ace is becoming much more dependable with his berm work & transition to NV. Turning between and going along islands is still giving him problems, crossing islands he's beginning to understand. Let's plan to work islands a couple more times to build his confidence, maybe use a drag to help him.

SAMPLE TRAINING MAP
Exercise 10

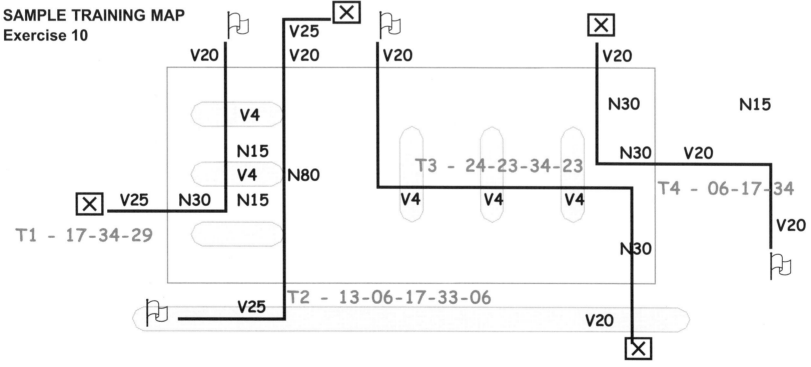

■ Advanced Training - **Incorporating Fence, Hedge & Wall Components**
■ **Exercise 11**

Exercise	11 - Incorporating Fence, Hedge & Wall Components.
Location	Grass area with hedges and/or fences.
Type of Location	Business/Industrial Park, Campus, School or Church, Office Building
Surfaces	Multiple
Components	As selected
Lesson Plan	Lay the components selected as diagramed. Continue to work the components in this exercise until your dog is confident working these scenting and surface transition problems and you are becoming comfortable with reading your dog's track indications.
Comments	Start yardage should be a minimum of 20 yards to transition area or turn. Continue all legs a minimum of 10 yards past transition areas or turns before ending the exercise.
	Review the section on "Fence, Hedge and Wall Components" (Chapter 21) of *Mastering Variable Surface Tracking: The Component Training Approach* for information on the effect various types of fence material and construction may have on the scent from a track in their vicinity.

Exercise 11 Incorporating Fence, Hedge & Wall Components Diagram

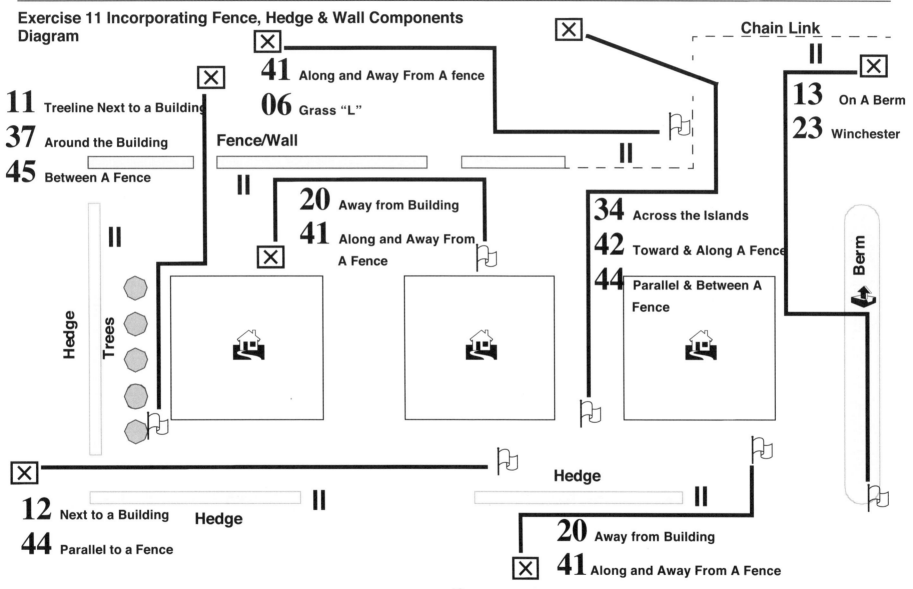

41 Along and Away From A fence

11 Treeline Next to a Building

06 Grass "L"

37 Around the Building

Fence/Wall

45 Between A Fence

20 Away from Building

41 Along and Away From A Fence

Hedge

Trees

Chain Link

13 On A Berm

23 Winchester

34 Across the Islands

42 Toward & Along A Fence

44 Parallel & Between A Fence

Berm

12 Next to a Building

Hedge

44 Parallel to a Fence

Hedge

20 Away from Building

41 Along and Away From A Fence

49

TRACKING NOTES

Date: 4/29/00 ☐ AM ✓ PM ✓ Day ☐ Night   Dog: Ace, Border Collie
Location: City College, Science Lab Buildings
Area Description: hedges and trees near buildings
Tracklayer: Heather Jones   Handler: Suzie Smith   TL Started: 6:35pm   Dog Started: 9:15pm

Ground Conditions: low grass, dry   Weather Conditions: dry   Wind Spd: 15mph   Temp: 73°
Components Utilized: 01, 06, 10, 11, 12, 35, 36, 37, 39, 42, 44, 45
Surfaces: grass   asphalt   cement   _____   _____   _____
Articles: ✓Fabric ✓Leather ✓Plastic ✓Metal
Comments: Missed both metal articles (work art. indication). Had problems working between trees and buildings, wind and building shadow may have pushed him through the trees. Seemed very confused around openings in walls, must work this exercise again in lighter wind.

SAMPLE TRAINING MAP
Exercise 11

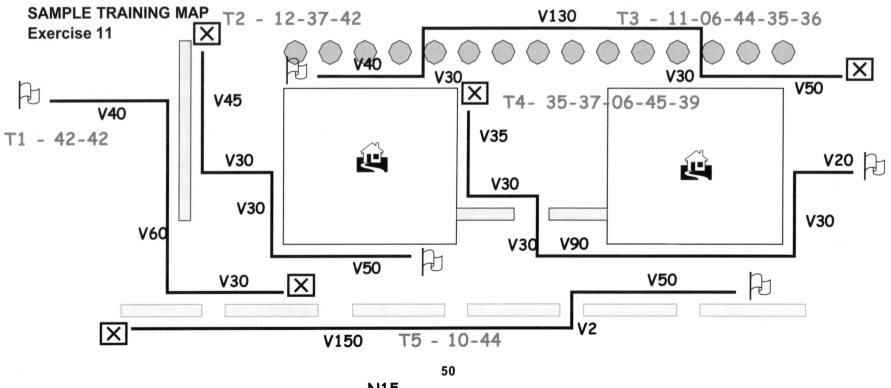

TRACKING NOTES

Date: 5/06/00 ✓ AM ☐ PM ✓ Day ☐ Night   Dog: Ace, Border Collie
Location: City College, Sports Training Area
Area Description: mowed lawn surroundng building & tennis court. Hedges and chain link fencing.
Tracklayer: Suzie Smith   Handler: Suzie Smith   TL Started: 7:12am   Dog Started: 9:35am
Ground Conditions: lawn   Weather Conditions: clear, sunny   Wind Spd: 3mph   Temp: 81°
Components Utilized: 01, 06, 11, 23, 35, 36, 42, 44, 45, 46
Surfaces: grass   asphalt   cement   _____   _____   _____
Articles: ✓Fabric   ✓Leather   ✓Plastic   ✓Metal
Comments: T1 - worked hedges nicely, very hesitant to enter tennis courts. I talked with 2 children playing and they stopped while I helped him across the tennis court. Must try this again on empty courts. T2 - Track started down-wind, chain link sucked him in and held him next to fence. Needs more work. T3/T4 problems with open turns.

SAMPLE TRAINING MAP
Exercise 11
Chain Link

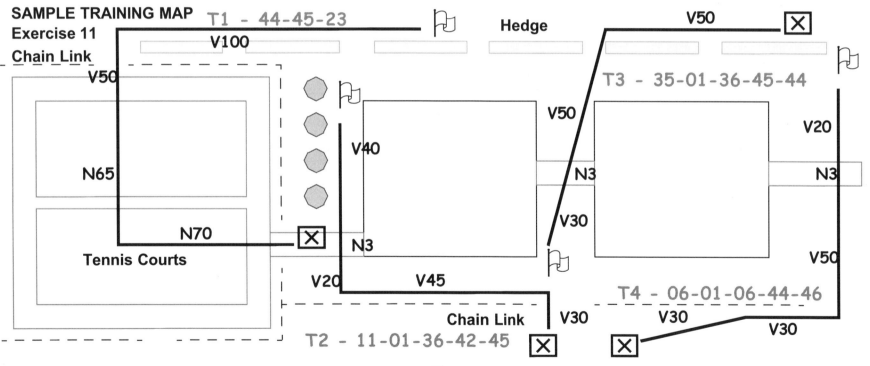

■ **Advanced Training - Incorporating Curbs & Gutter Components**
■ **Exercise 12**

Exercise	12 - Incorporating Curbs & Gutter Components
Location	Streets with curbs and/or gutters, parking lots with islands.
Type of Location	Business/Industrial Park, Campus, School or Church, Office Building
Surfaces	Multiple
Components	As Selected
Lesson Plan	Lay the components selected as diagramed. Continue to work the components in this exercise until your dog is confident working these scenting and surface transition problems and you are becoming comfortable with reading your dog's track indications.
Comments	Start yardage should be a minimum of 20 yards to transition area or turn. Continue all legs a minimum of 10 yards past transition areas or turns before ending the exercise.
	Curbs and gutters accumulate track scent. Your dog may work along the curb or gutter following blown scent rather than the actual track. It may be beneficial in your training to utilize drags and/or handprints to help your dog through these components.

Exercise 12 Incorporating Curbs & Gutter Components
Diagram

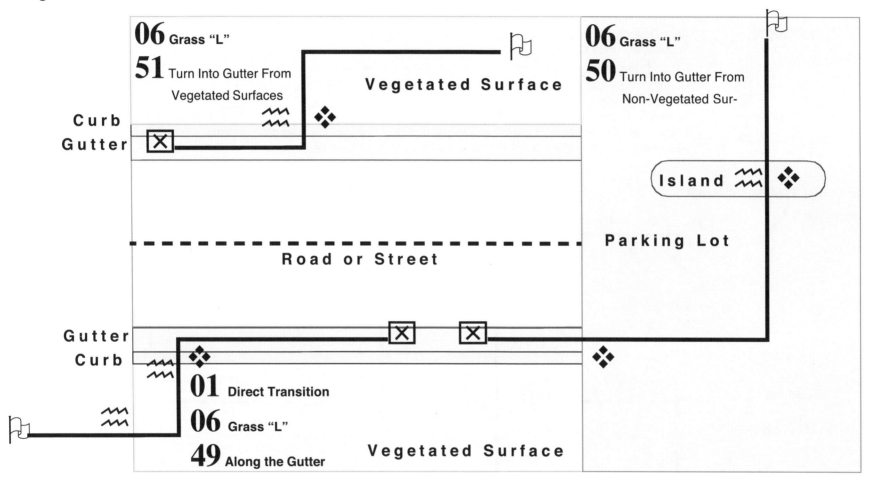

TRACKING NOTES

Date: 5/13/00 ✓ AM ☐ PM ✓ Day ☐ Night   Dog: Ace, Border Collie

Location: Northwest Industrial Park - Geotech Services entry road

Area Description: short grass, city street, curbs and gutters.

Tracklayer: Judy Collins   Handler: Suzie Smith   TL Started: 8:03am   Dog Started:11:20am

Ground Conditions: low grass, dry   Weather Conditions: hot, dry   Wind Spd: 12mph   Temp: 87°

Components Utilized: 01, 06, 50

Surfaces: grass   asphalt   cement   _____   _____   _____

Articles: ✓Fabric ✓Leather   ✓Plastic ✓Metal

Comments: Handled street crossings without a problem, worked up and down gutters, missed first turn in gutter, but with encouragement came back to find it. Will need lots of work in this area.

SAMPLE TRAINING MAP
Exercise 12

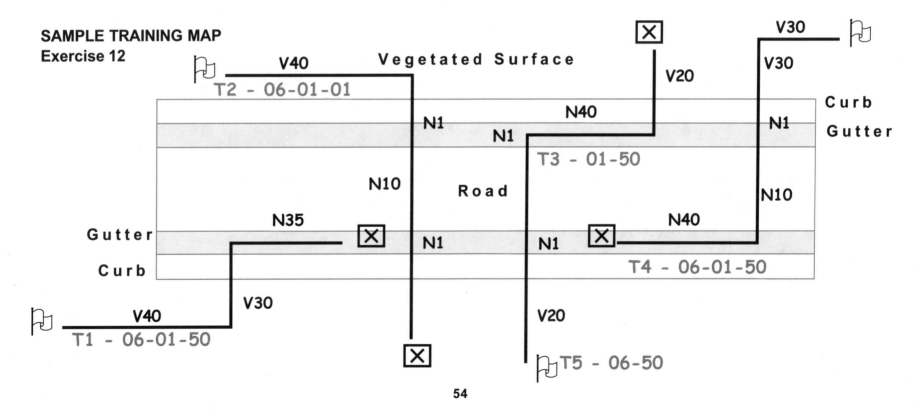

TRACKING NOTES

Date: 5/20/00 ✓ AM ☐ PM ✓ Day ☐ Night   Dog: Ace, Border Collie

Location: Northwest Industrial Park - Geotech Services entry road

Area Description: short grass, city street, curbs and gutters.

Tracklayer: Judy Collins   Handler: Suzie Smith   TL Started: 6:33am   Dog Started: 9:17am

Ground Conditions: low grass, wet   Weather Conditions: rain   Wind Spd: 12mph   Temp: 67°

Components Utilized: 01, 23, 50, 51

Surfaces: grass   asphalt   stone   concrete   _____   _____

Articles: ✓Fabric   ✓Leather   ✓Plastic   ✓Metal

Comments: Relaid last week's tracks, this time in rain. Water running in gutters wiped out track. Ace followed scent down gutter 90 yds, to first drain. Swore to us that Judy climbed down drain. Took him back to corner and worked slowly until he found the track. T4 - same problem as above, threw down article & ended track.   Playtime.

SAMPLE TRAINING MAP
Exercise 12

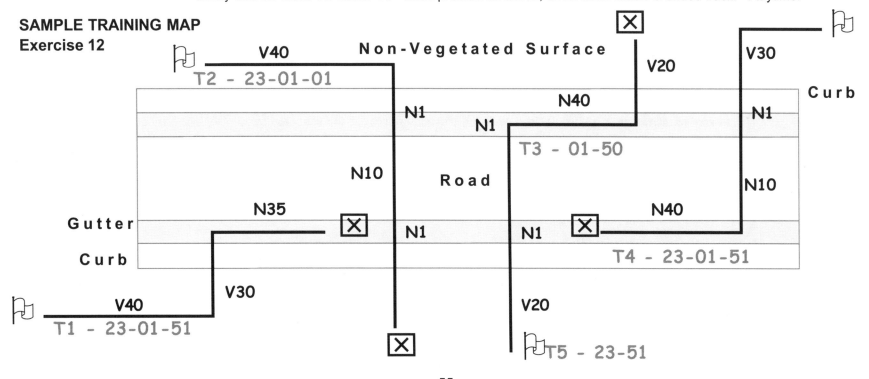

■ Advanced Training - **Incorporating Elevation Components**
■ **Exercise 13**

Exercise	13 - Incorporating Elevation Components
Location	Berms and landscaping around buildings
Type of Location	Business/Industrial Park, Campus, School or Church, Office Building
Surfaces	Multiple
Components	As selected
Lesson Plan	Lay the components selected as diagramed. Continue to work the components in this exercise until your dog is confident working these scenting and surface transition problems and you are becoming comfortable with reading your dog's track indications.
Comments	Start yardage should be a minimum of 20 yards to transition area or turn. Continue all legs a minimum of 10 yards past transition areas or turns before ending the exercise.
	The scent from the track in these components is affected in three ways: the building shadow will tend to pull or push the scent toward or away from the building itself while the elevation will cause the scent to flow downhill, and vegetation of the landscaping will collect the scent as it flows.

Exercise 13 Incorporating Elevation Components
Diagram

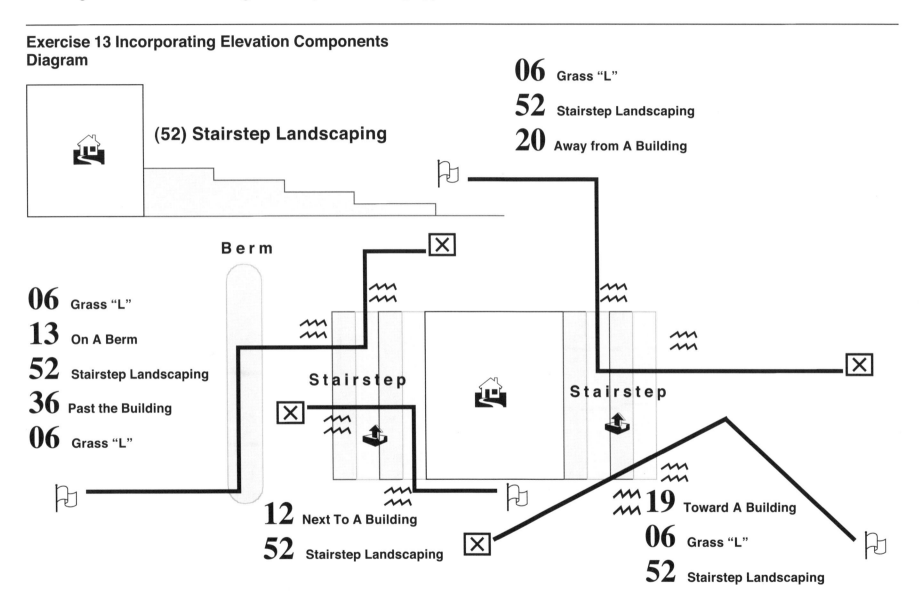

06 Grass "L"

52 Stairstep Landscaping

20 Away from A Building

(52) Stairstep Landscaping

B e r m

06 Grass "L"

13 On A Berm

52 Stairstep Landscaping

36 Past the Building

06 Grass "L"

S t a i r s t e p

S t a i r s t e p

12 Next To A Building

52 Stairstep Landscaping

19 Toward A Building

06 Grass "L"

52 Stairstep Landscaping

Exercise 13 Incorporating Elevation Components
Diagram

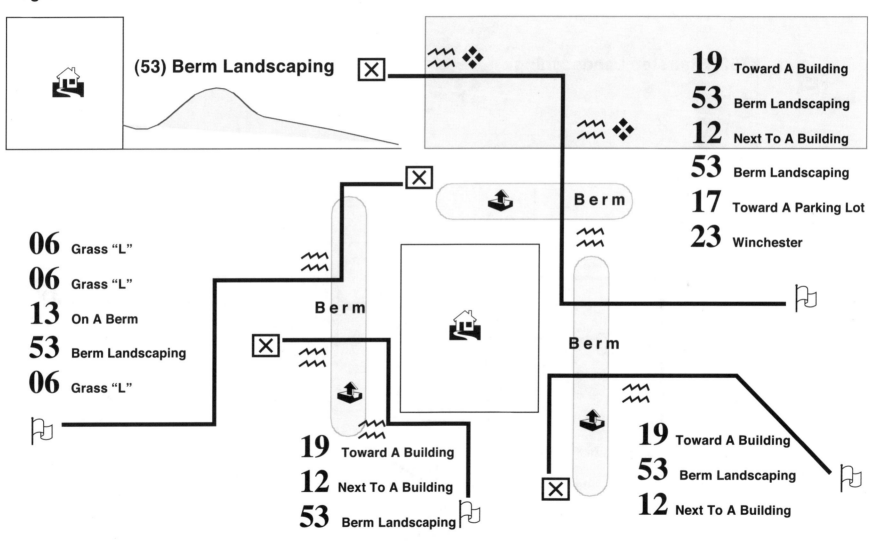

Exercise 13 Incorporating Elevation Components Diagram

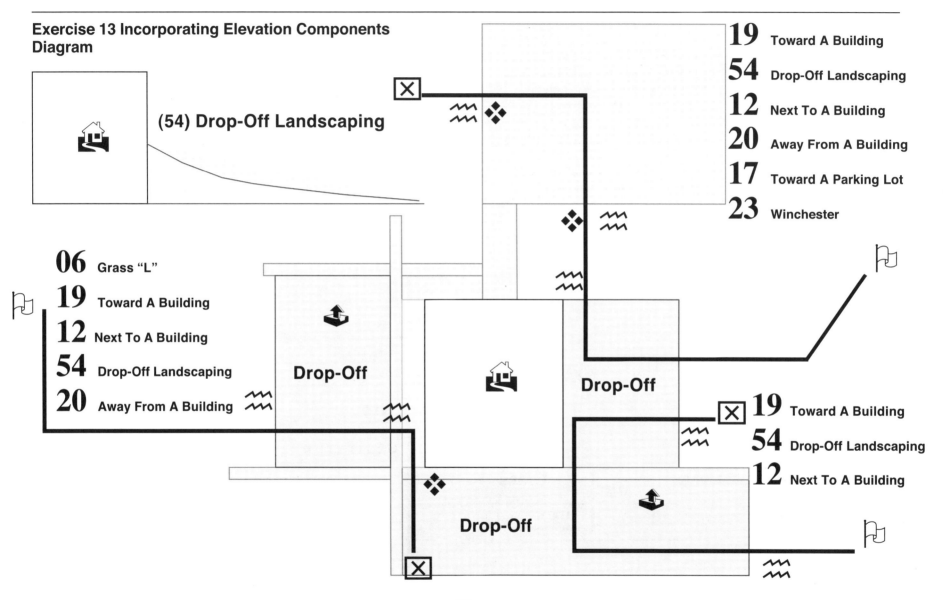

(54) Drop-Off Landscaping

19 Toward A Building
54 Drop-Off Landscaping
12 Next To A Building
20 Away From A Building
17 Toward A Parking Lot
23 Winchester

06 Grass "L"
19 Toward A Building
12 Next To A Building
54 Drop-Off Landscaping
20 Away From A Building

Drop-Off

Drop-Off

Drop-Off

19 Toward A Building
54 Drop-Off Landscaping
12 Next To A Building

TRACKING NOTES

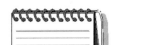

Date: 5/27/00 ✓ AM ☐ PM ✓ Day ☐ Night   Dog: Ace, Border Collie
Location: New Covenant Church
Area Description: Church grounds, berms, islands, parking lot
Tracklayer: Judy Collins   Handler: Suzie Smith   TL Started: 6:33am   Dog Started: 9:17am
Ground Conditions: low grass, dry   Weather Conditions: rain   Wind Spd: 25mph   Temp: 67°
Components Utilized: 01, 06, 13, 14, 19, 35, 38, 39, 52
Surfaces: grass   asphalt   mulch   _____   _____   _____
Articles: ✓Fabric ✓Leather ✓Plastic ✓Metal
Comments: Smell from mulch made him parallel the track. Did not seem to want to go up the landscaping levels.
Once out of mulch, worked rest of track without problem. Need to work lots of mulch and stairstep landscaping.

SAMPLE TRAINING MAP
Exercise 13

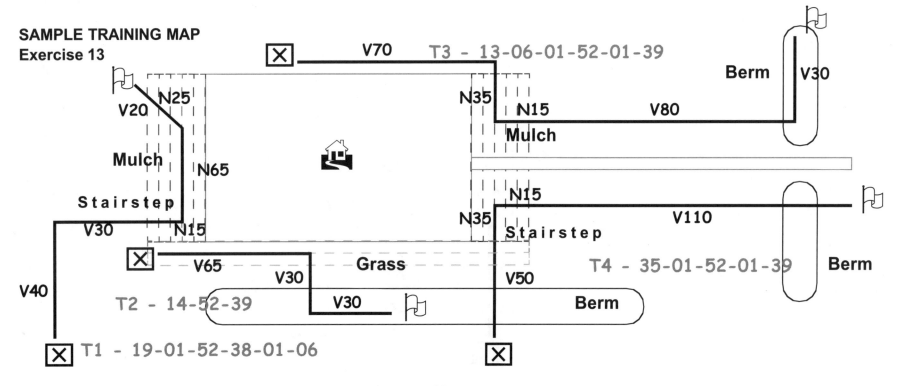

TRACKING NOTES

Date: 6/03/00 ✓ AM ☐ PM ✓ Day ☐ Night   Dog: Ace, Border Collie
Location: Premier Refractories
Area Description: Building with berms, trees, hedges, sidewalk
Tracklayer: Suzie Smith   Handler: Suzie Smith   TL Started: 7:18am   Dog Started: 9:22am
Ground Conditions: low grass, dry   Weather Conditions: sunny, hot   Wind Spd: 2mph   Temp: 84°
Components Utilized: 01, 06, 07, 09, 11, 35, 38, 39, 53
Surfaces: grass   asphalt   cement   _____ _____ _____
Articles: ✓Fabric ✓Leather ✓Plastic ✓Metal
Comments: Swirling winds close to building caused initial problem working on berms. Seemed to be sometimes
pulled to building or pushed away on the same leg. Moved up on line and slowed him down and he stayed much
closer to track. Cutting across berms is going to take more practice. T2 - tried to cut off first corner and go directly to
the berm following the drifting scent.

SAMPLE TRAINING MAP
Exercise 13

T1 - 35-06-53-38-06-01-07-09

V60

V30

V100

Berm   T3 - 35-11-06-53-53

V30

V30   V60

N3   N3

V40

V50

Hedge   V30

V40   Berm

T2 - 06-53-39-01   V70

V30

V90

61

Mastering Variable Surface Tracking: The Component Training Approach Workbook

---

TRACKING NOTES

Date: 6/10/00 ✓ AM ☐ PM ✓ Day ☐ Night   Dog: Ace, Border Collie
Location: First Baptist Church
Area Description: Local church grounds, lawns, brick sidewalks
Tracklayer: Heather Jones   Handler: Suzie Smith   TL Started: 625am   Dog Started: 10:05am
Ground Conditions: low grass, dry   Weather Conditions: cloudy, humid   Wind Spd: 5mph   Temp: 86°
Components Utilized: 01, 06, 07, 35, 36, 38, 39, 54
Surfaces: grass   brick   cement _____ _____ _____
Articles: ✓Fabric ✓Leather ✓Plastic ✓Metal
Comments: Church sits on top of a man-made 20 ft hill. Most of the track is either up-hill or down-hill. Ace has less trouble on the up-hill legs than on the down-hill where it appears the scent is drifting in a much wider pattern. By shortening up on the lead on the down-hill legs, was able to keep Ace close to the track. This is a real challenge.

SAMPLE TRAINING MAP
Exercise 13

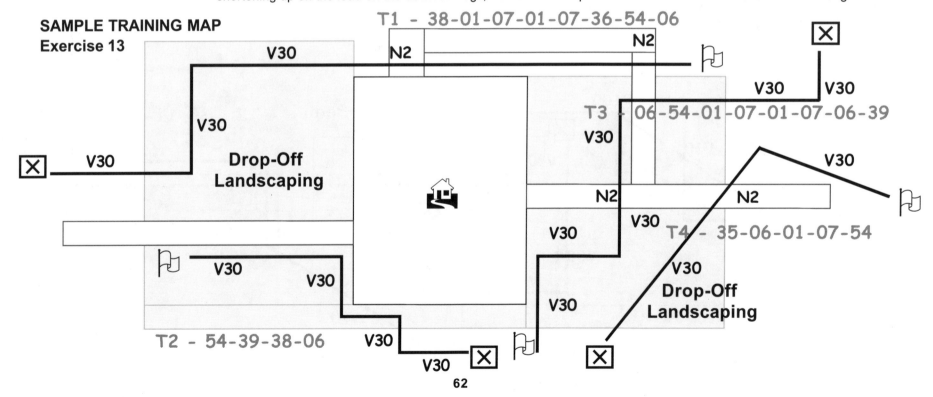

62

■ Advanced Training - Incorporating Alleys & Walkway Components
■ Exercise 14

Exercise	14 - Incorporating Alleys & Walkway Components
Location	Walkways near and between buildings or paralleling roadways or parking lots
Type of Location	Business/Industrial Park, Campus, School or Church, Office Building
Surfaces	Multiple
Components	As selected
Lesson Plan	Lay the components selected as diagramed. Continue to work the components in this exercise until your dog is confident working these scenting and surface transition problems and you are becoming comfortable with reading your dog's track indications.
Comments	Start yardage should be a minimum of 20 yards to transition area or turn. Continue all legs a minimum of 10 yards past transition areas or turns before ending the exercise.

When working near or between buildings, keep in mind that you are working within the building shadow and that wind swirls between the buildings creating a tunnel effect. Article placement within these areas is critical. In confined spaces, your dog may work against the building or slightly away from the track and could miss an article in this area. As a handler and a team member you should always be observant in assisting your dog in the search for articles.

Exercise 14 Incorporating Alleys & Walkway Components
Diagram

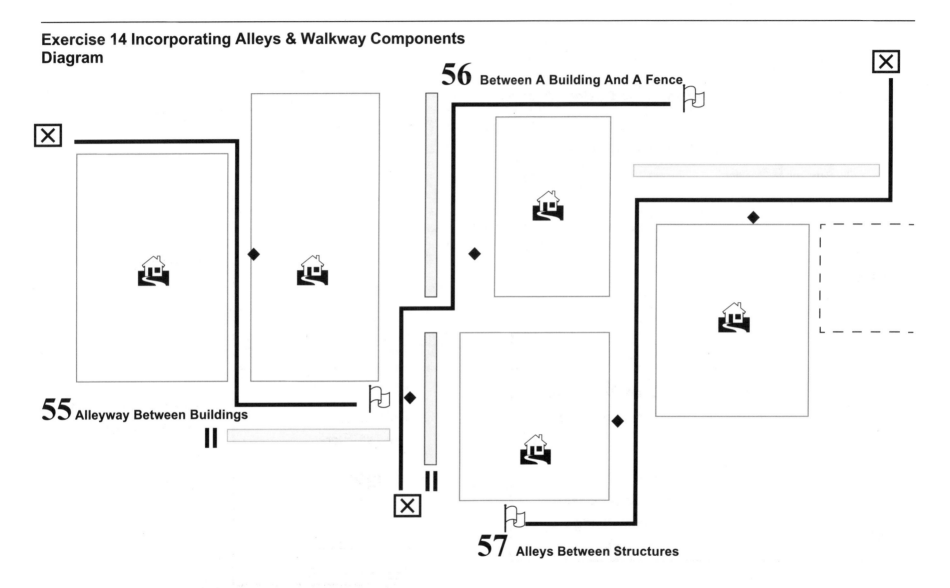

56 Between A Building And A Fence

55 Alleyway Between Buildings

57 Alleys Between Structures

Exercise 14 Incorporating Alleys & Walkway Components
Diagram

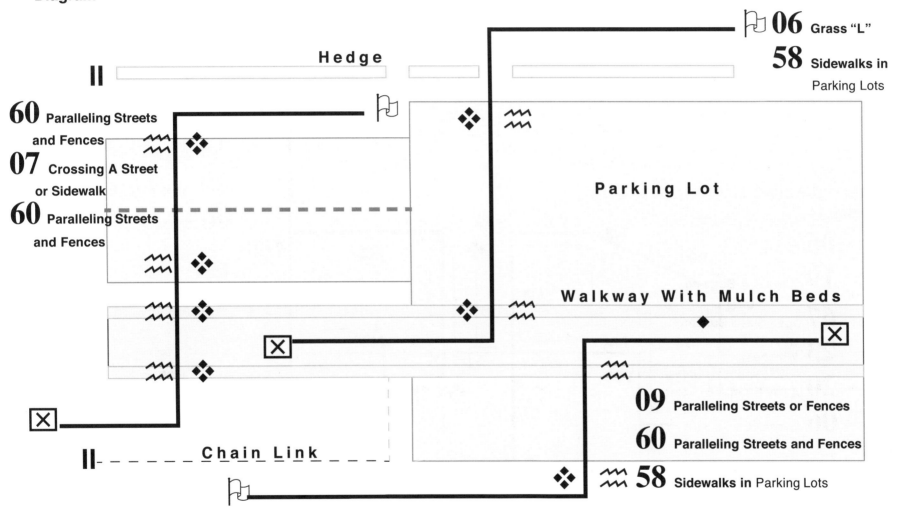

TRACKING NOTES

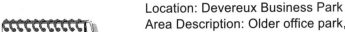

Date: 6/17/00 ✓ AM ☐ PM ✓ Day ☐ Night   Dog: Ace, Border Collie
Location: Devereux Business Park
Area Description: Older office park, mainly wooden buildings, gravel and stone walkways, concrete sidewalks
Tracklayer: Judy Collins   Handler: Suzie Smith   TL Started: 6:31am   Dog Started: 9:45am
Ground Conditions: low grass, wet   Weather Conditions: drizzle   Wind Spd: 10mph   Temp: 74°
Components Utilized: 01, 06, 07, 08, 16, 19, 20, 35, 38, 39, 45, 55, 56, 57, 59
Surfaces: grass   stone   gravel   concrete   _____   _____
Articles: ✓Fabric ✓Leather   ✓Plastic ✓Metal
Comments: Narrow paths, mature landscaping and trees, created a tunnel effect between the buildings. Ace
checked each entrance way and sometimes seemed to be pulled 10-15 yds into the tunnel before backing out and
continuing on track. Need to work on walkways between buildings again. Not happy with overall performance.

SAMPLE TRAINING MAP
Exercise 14

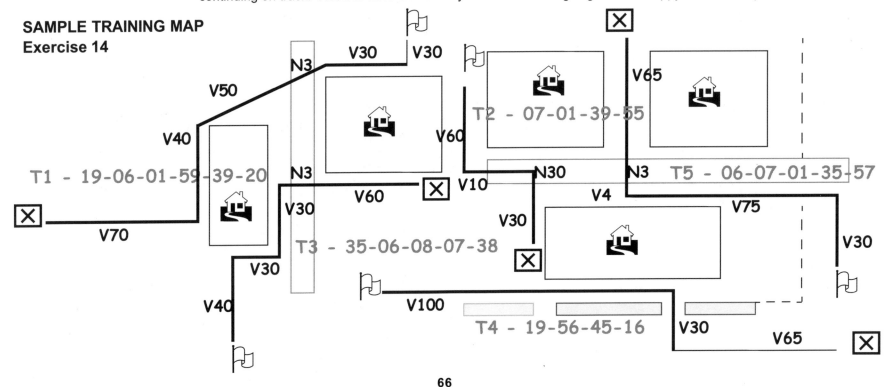

TRACKING NOTES

Date: 6/24/00 ✓ AM ☐ PM ✓ Day ☐ Night   Dog: Ace, Border Collie
Location: Bellweather Electrical Components
Area Description: Multi-building private electronic company
Tracklayer: Suzie Smith   Handler: Suzie Smith   TL Started: 7:03am   Dog Started: 9:57am
Ground Conditions: low grass, wet   Weather Conditions: rain   Wind Spd: 15mph   Temp: 77°
Components Utilized: 06, 19, 20, 35, 36, 38, 39, 40, 41, 42, 43, 55, 56
Surfaces: grass   asphalt   gravel   sand   mulch   _____
Articles: ✓Fabric ✓Leather ✓Plastic ✓Metal
Comments: Ace worked much better between the buildings, casted back and forth between building and tall wall. Handled working around buildings very nicely, corners were sharp, track indication is getting much better. Very fun place to track, need to bring Judy and Heather here (with their dogs).

SAMPLE TRAINING MAP
Exercise 14

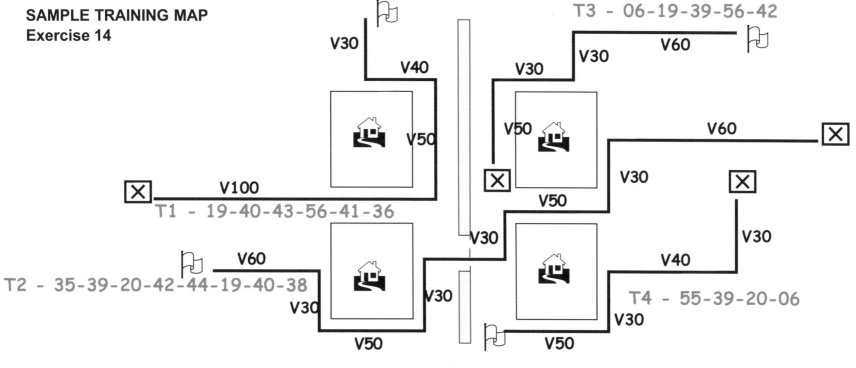

TRACKING NOTES

Date: 7/01/00   ✓ AM ☐ PM ✓ Day ☐ Night   Dog: Ace, Border Collie

Location: Walker Convalescent Home

Area Description: Wide raised walkways, no curbs, all walkway surfaces wheelchair accessible

Tracklayer: Judy Collins   Handler: Suzie Smith   TL Started: 6:02am   Dog Started: 7:40am

Ground Conditions: low grass, dry   Weather Conditions: cloudy, cool   Wind Spd: 5mph   Temp: 63°

Components Utilized: 01, 06, 07, 08, 12, 18, 19, 20, 28, 36, 39 40, 59, 60

Surfaces: grass   asphalt   concrete _____   _____   _____

Articles: ✓Fabric ✓Leather   ✓Plastic ✓Metal

Comments: Ace approached several times on track by people with walkers or wheelchairs. His therapy training kicked in and he patiently sat while each person petted him. Had difficulty on the sloped edges of the walkways, but worked nicely through the parking lot.

SAMPLE TRAINING MAP
Exercise 14

T1 - 36-01-07-01-59-39-20

T2 - 12-01-07-06-01-08-01-28-01-19

T4 - 19-60-40-59

T3 - 18-06-01-07-01-39

V40 V30 V10 V60 N10 V25 V50 V30 V50 V15 N25 N15 V20 N25 V30 V30 N2 V30 V20 N10 V4 V20 V40 N10 V4 V15

TRACKING NOTES

Date: 7/08/00 ☐ AM ✓ PM ☐ Day ✓ Night   Dog: Ace, Border Collie
Location: County Court complex
Area Description: Main parking lot walkway with wide mulch beds and broken hedges
Tracklayer: Bob Smith   Handler: Suzie Smith   TL Started: 7:40pm   Dog Started: 10:09pm

Ground Conditions: low grass, dry   Weather Conditions: clear   Wind Spd: 3mph   Temp: 61°
Components Utilized: 01, 07, 23, 27, 32, 45, 58, 70
Surfaces: mulch   asphalt   stone   dirt   grass   _____
Articles: ✓Fabric ✓Leather   ✓Plastic ✓Metal
Comments: Could sure see improvement in Ace's article indication after we played the Article Game several times. Crossing the mulch, the walk, and through the hedges seemed easy, yet when turning on the walk Ace overshot the turn everytime. Will need to work on this component many more times, but it is an easy one and quick to lay.

**SAMPLE TRAINING MAP
Exercise 14**

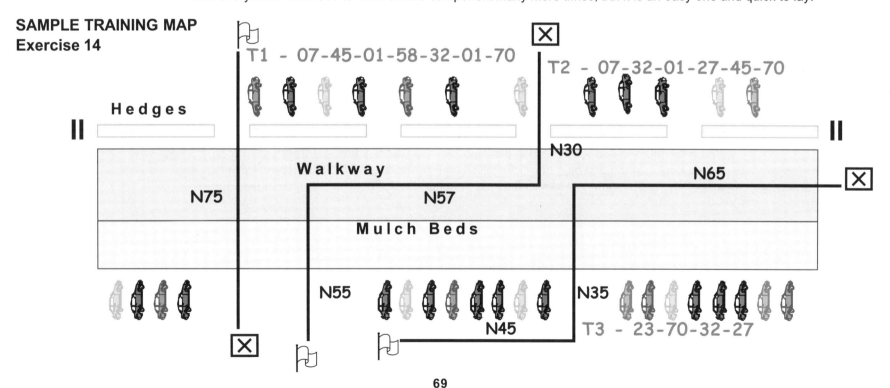

■ **Advanced Training** - **Incorporating Water Components**
■ **Exercise 15**

Exercise	15 - Incorporating Water Components
Location	Streets and parking lots with water collected along gutters, in puddles and sprinkler run-off.
Type of Location	Business/Industrial Park, Campus, School or Church, Office Building
Surfaces	Multiple
Components	As selected
Lesson Plan	Lay the components selected as diagramed. Continue to work the components in this exercise until your dog is confident working these scenting and surface transition problems and you are becoming comfortable with reading your dog's track indications.
Comments	Start yardage should be a minimum of 20 yards to transition area or turn. Continue all legs a minimum of 10 yards past transition areas or turns before ending the exercise.

On tracks laid in these areas, the scent will be drawn toward the water and will spread out along the surface and collect along the edges. As your dog follows the track, he may be drawn to the water's edge and give you his indication for loss of track. Allow your dog to search these areas, while watching him for his indications. Encourage your dog to remain near the track. You may return to find articles left in this area are now wet or under water with their scent flowing many yards away from the actual track. At the first sign of article indication by your dog, stand your ground, give him line, use your "magic words" and allow him the opportunity to search the area thoroughly.

Exercise 15 Incorporating Water Components Diagram

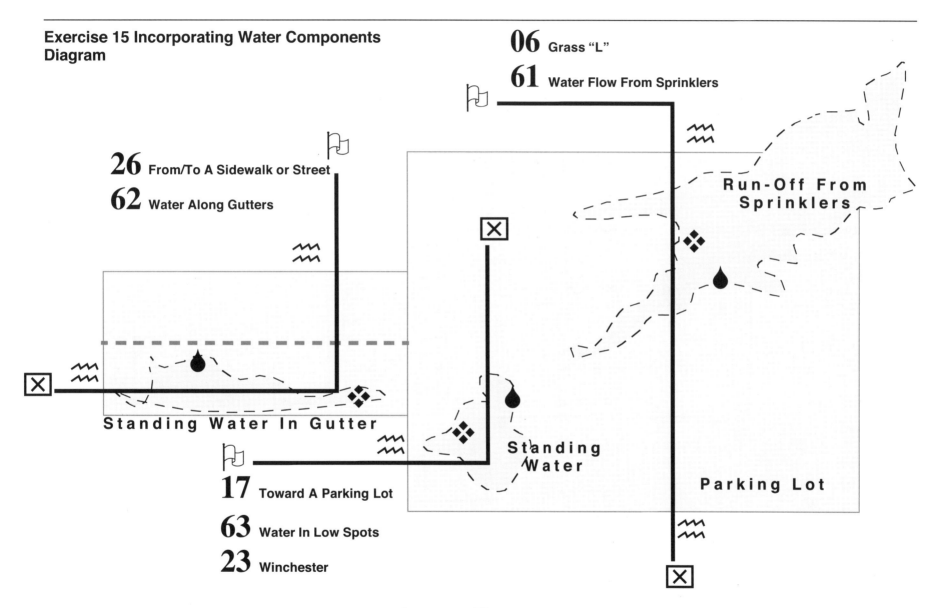

06 Grass "L"

61 Water Flow From Sprinklers

26 From/To A Sidewalk or Street

62 Water Along Gutters

Run-Off From Sprinklers

Standing Water In Gutter

Standing Water

Parking Lot

17 Toward A Parking Lot

63 Water In Low Spots

23 Winchester

TRACKING NOTES

Date: 7/22/00 ✓ AM☐ PM ✓ Day ☐ Night   Dog: Ace, Border Collie

Location: Northwest Industrial Park dead end road

Area Description: double lane concrete road with curbs and gutters, standing water from recent rains

Tracklayer: Heather Jones   Handler: Suzie Smith   TL Started: 6:41am   Dog Started: 10:13am

Ground Conditions: standing water   Weather Conditions: sunny, hot, humid   Wind Spd: 5mph   Temp: 87°

Components Utilized: 01, 06, 23, 29, 49, 50, 51

Surfaces: grass   concrete   dirt   gravel   _____   _____

Articles: ✓Fabric ✓Leather   ✓Plastic ✓Metal

Comments: T1 - crossing water no problem. T2 - overshot first corner, worked along curb and found track, overshot second corner. T3 - Walked over first article (it was in the water), followed scent from article down to corner, helped him come back to locate article. T4 - overshot corner, paralleled road. Need to work on this.

SAMPLE TRAINING MAP
Exercise 15

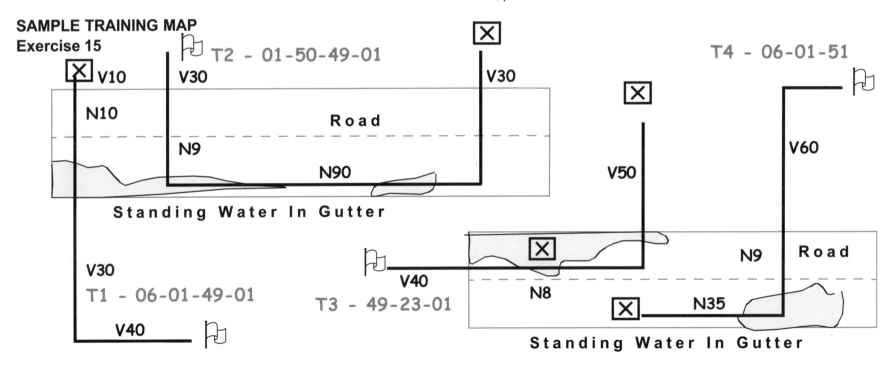

TRACKING NOTES

Date: 7/29/00 ☐ AM ✓ PM ☐ Day ✓ Night   Dog: Ace, Border Collie
Location: City College parking lot "Q"
Area Description: well-lit parking area, broken asphalt, standing water, run-off from surrounding sprinklers
Tracklayer: Bob Smith   Handler: Suzie Smith   TL Started: 9:55pm   Dog Started: 2:13am

Ground Conditions: standing water   Weather Conditions: cloudy, windy   Wind Spd: 4mph   Temp: 68°
Components Utilized: 01, 06, 17, 23, 61, 63
Surfaces: grass   asphalt   gravel _____   _____   _____
Articles: ✓Fabric ✓Leather   ✓Plastic ✓Metal
Comments: Ace worked the fringes of the standing water on the first couple of tracks, apparently following flowing scent. By T3, was venturing into the water close to the actual track. The scent appears to spread out across the surface of the standing water whenever the tracklayer walks through standing water. Another area that will require additional work! Really fun working at 2am.

SAMPLE TRAINING MAP
Exercise 15

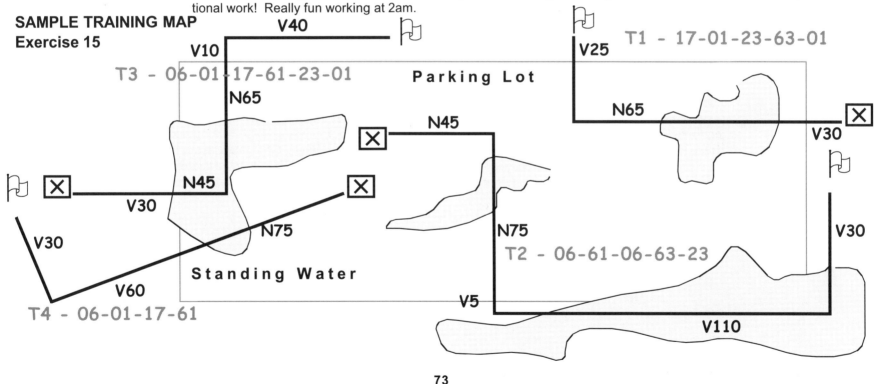

■ Advanced Training - **Incorporating Stairs & Ramp Components**
■ **Exercise 16**

Exercise	16 - Incorporating Stairs & Ramp Components
Location	Buildings with stairs and ramps
Type of Location	Business/Industrial Park, Campus, School or Church, Office Building
Surfaces	Multiple
Components	As selected
Lesson Plan	Lay the components selected as diagramed. Continue to work the components in this exercise until your dog is confident working these scenting and surface transition problems and you are becoming comfortable with reading your dog's track indications.
Comments	Start yardage should be a minimum of 20 yards to transition area or turn. Continue all legs a minimum of 10 yards past transition areas or turns before ending the exercise.
	Keep safety in mind when working around these components. Encourage your dog to work these slowly and methodically to prevent endangering you, your dog, or other pedestrians. Closed back risers typically found as elevation components or leading to the entrances of buildings, tend to collect the scent at the back of the steps. Working across a set of wide steps may cause initial confusion to your dog in determining the exact area of the track. Open back risers tend to allow the scent to flow off of the steps and onto the surface below the stairs, sometimes causing the dog to investigate under the stairs before determining track direction. When working ramps, depending on the height of the ramp, the dog may work parallel to the ramp rather than on the ramp itself.

Exercise 16 Incorporating Stairs & Ramp Components
Diagram
Closed Back Risers (Stairs)

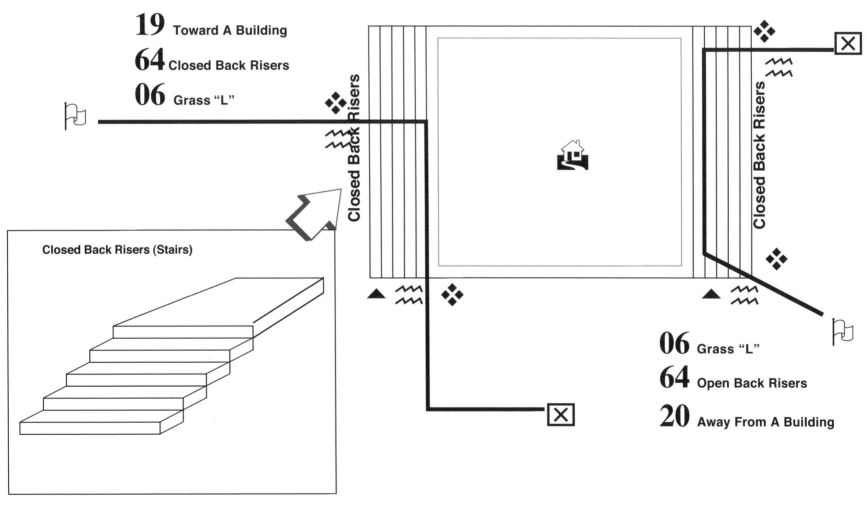

19 Toward A Building

64 Closed Back Risers

06 Grass "L"

Closed Back Risers

Closed Back Risers

Closed Back Risers (Stairs)

06 Grass "L"

64 Open Back Risers

20 Away From A Building

Exercise 16 Incorporating Stairs & Ramp Components
Diagram
Open Back Risers (Stairs)

Typically found as staircases to second floor or to raised walkways

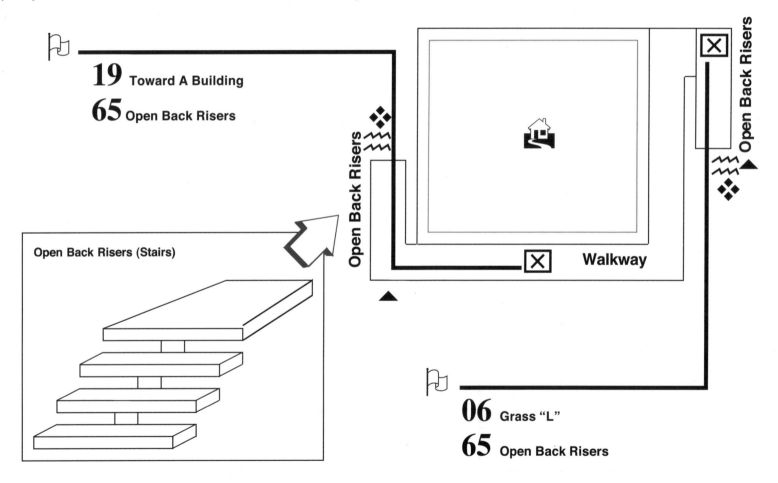

19 Toward A Building

65 Open Back Risers

Open Back Risers (Stairs)

Open Back Risers

Open Back Risers

Walkway

06 Grass "L"

65 Open Back Risers

Exercise 16 Incorporating Stairs & Ramp Components
Diagram
Wheelchair Ramps

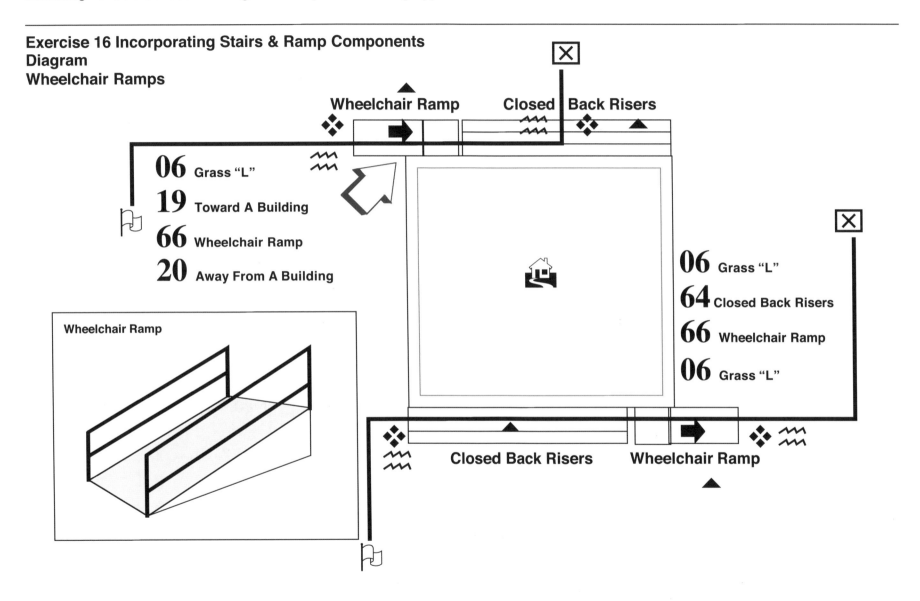

Wheelchair Ramp

Closed Back Risers

06 Grass "L"
19 Toward A Building
66 Wheelchair Ramp
20 Away From A Building

Wheelchair Ramp

06 Grass "L"
64 Closed Back Risers
66 Wheelchair Ramp
06 Grass "L"

Closed Back Risers   Wheelchair Ramp

TRACKING NOTES

Date: 8/06/00 ✓ AM☐ PM ✓ Day ☐ Night   Dog: Ace, Border Collie

Location: First National Bank

Area Description: Building with multiple closed back risers, wheelchair ramps

Tracklayer: Heather Jones   Handler: Suzie Smith   TL Started: 7:17am   Dog Started: 10:21am

Ground Conditions: , dry   Weather Conditions: sunny, hot   Wind Spd: 0mph   Temp: 91°

Components Utilized: 01, 06, 07, 09, 32, 38, 64

Surfaces: grass   asphalt   concrete   brick   _____   _____

Articles: ✓Fabric   ✓Leather   ✓Plastic   ✓Metal

Comments: T1 - first set of stairs, no problem. Going down second set, Ace followed scent across the front of the building and initially went down wheelchair ramp. Backed up and worked through the problem. Same basic problems on next two tracks.

SAMPLE TRAINING MAP

Exercise 16

Closed Back Risers

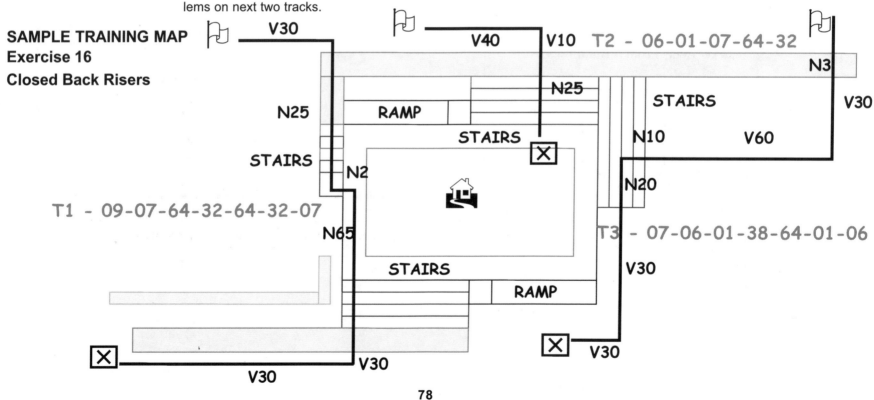

TRACKING NOTES

Date: 8/12/00 ✓ AM ☐ PM ✓ Day ☐ Night   Dog: Ace, Border Collie

Location: Architectural Services

Area Description: Building with stone walkways, open back risers to building and over flowing creek

Tracklayer: Suzie Smith   Handler: Suzie Smith   TL Started: 6:29am   Dog Started:10:08am

Ground Conditions: dry   Weather Conditions: cloudy, warm   Wind Spd: 5mph   Temp: 85⁰

Components Utilized: 01, 06, 07, 39, 65

Surfaces: grass   stone   concrete   mulch   dirt   wood

Articles: ✓Fabric   ✓Leather   ✓Plastic   ✓Metal

Comments: Ace's initial reaction to the open risers was to try to search underneath them. After several minutes of searching, he returned to the track and crossed the bridge. Risers at building did not give him as much trouble. More work required on these components.

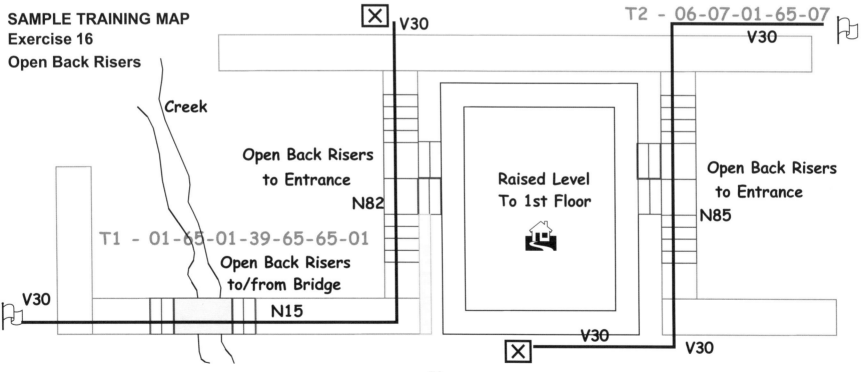

SAMPLE TRAINING MAP

Exercise 16

Open Back Risers

TRACKING NOTES

Date: 8/20/00 ✓ AM ☐ PM ✓ Day ☐ Night   Dog: Ace, Border Collie
Location: First National Bank
Area Description: Building with multiple closed back risers, wheelchair ramps
Tracklayer: Judy Collins   Handler: Suzie Smith   TL Started: 5:08am   Dog Started: 8:11am
Ground Conditions: dry   Weather Conditions: clear, sunny   Wind Spd: 4mph   Temp: 82°
Components Utilized: 01, 06, 19, 26, 27, 37, 64, 66
Surfaces: grass   asphalt   concrete   brick   _____   _____
Articles: ✓Fabric   ✓Leather   ✓Plastic   ✓Metal
Comments: Worked ramp properly, overshot every turn on stairs, must work more stairs.

SAMPLE TRAINING MAP
Exercise 16
Wheelchair Ramps

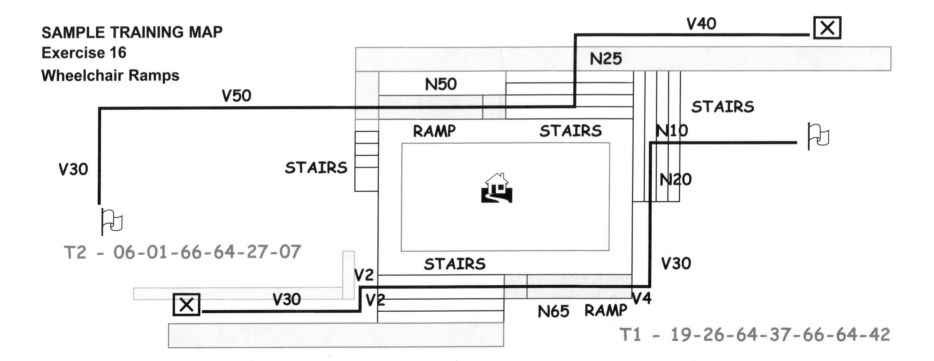

T2 - 06-01-66-64-27-07

T1 - 19-26-64-37-66-64-42

■ **Advanced Training - Incorporating Open Buildings & Garage Components**
■ **Exercise 17**

Exercise	17 - Incorporating Open Buildings & Garage Components
Location	Open sided buildings including pavillions and parking garages
Type of Location	Business/Industrial Park, Campus, School or Church, Office Building
Surfaces	Multiple
Components	As selected
Lesson Plan	Lay the components selected as diagramed. Continue to work the components in this exercise until your dog is confident working these scenting and surface transition problems and you are becoming comfortable with reading your dog's track indications.
Comments	Start yardage should be a minimum of 20 yards to transition area or turn. Continue all legs a minimum of 10 yards past transition areas or turns before ending the exercise.

Challenges facing you when working in or around open buildings, pavillions, walled courtyards and parking garages include swirling winds, blowing scent, typically polished floor surfaces, and an opportunity for dog to work outside the building while still being correct. Therefore article placement is critical. As a handler you should always be observant and a team member in assisting your dog in the search for articles. Always be alert for moving traffic in these areas; and expect to find some or all of your articles left in this area either moved or missing. Watch for oil, antifreeze, or other dangerous substances which may have leaked onto the surface. Floors inside covered structures tend to collect moisture and remain damp or wet, creating the potential for slips and falls.

81

Exercise 17 Incorporating Open Buildings & Garage Components
Diagram
Open Sided (Covered) Building
Basketball court, covered playground, covered parking, etc.

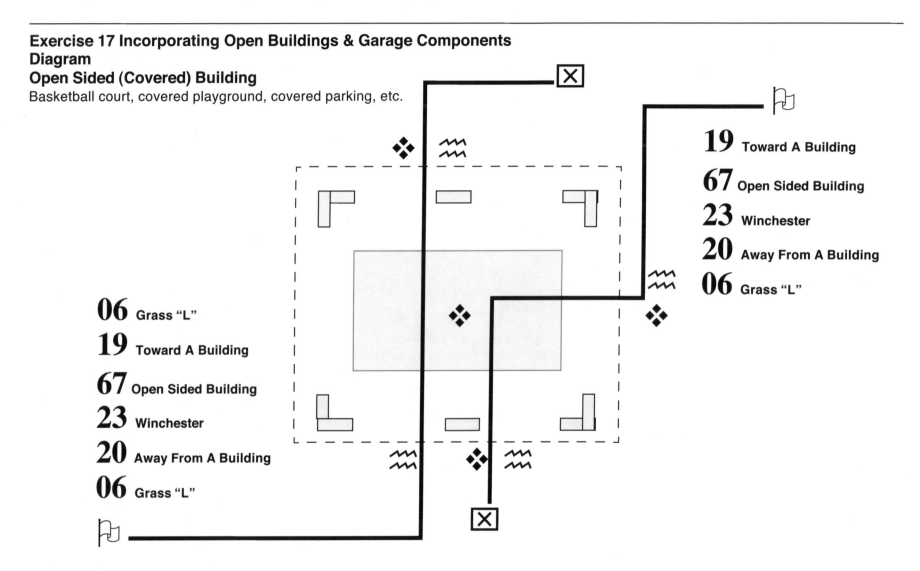

19 Toward A Building

67 Open Sided Building

23 Winchester

20 Away From A Building

06 Grass "L"

06 Grass "L"

19 Toward A Building

67 Open Sided Building

23 Winchester

20 Away From A Building

06 Grass "L"

Exercise 17 Incorporating Open Buildings & Garage Components Diagram
Pavilions

06 Grass "L"

19 Toward A Building

68 Pavilion

23 Winchester

20 Away From A Building

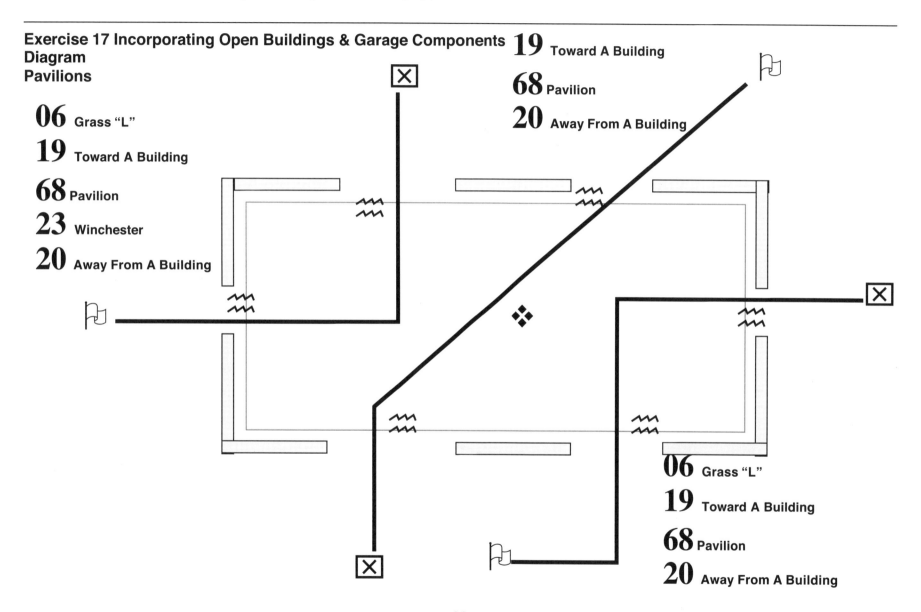

19 Toward A Building

68 Pavilion

20 Away From A Building

06 Grass "L"

19 Toward A Building

68 Pavilion

20 Away From A Building

Exercise 17 Incorporating Open Buildings & Garage Components
Diagram
Parking Garages

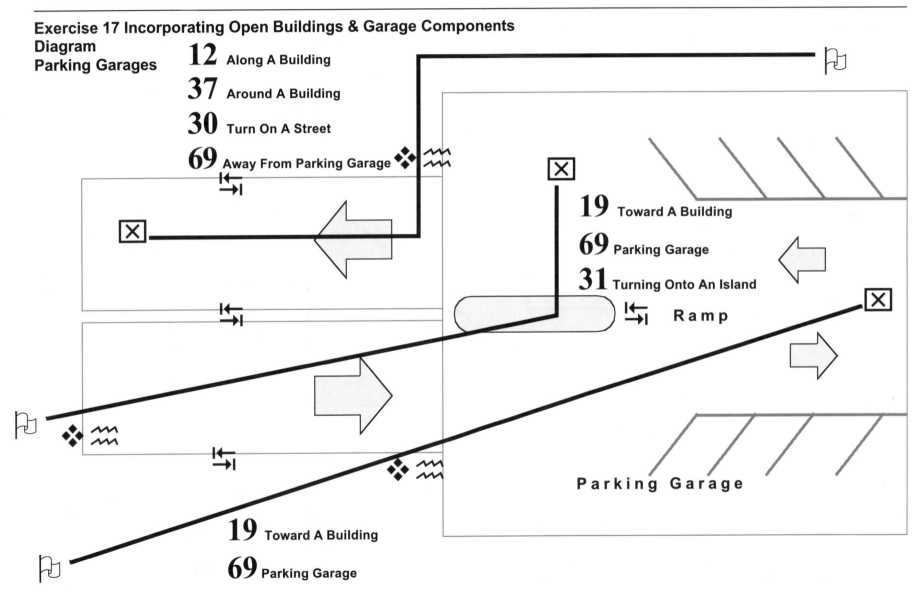

12 Along A Building

37 Around A Building

30 Turn On A Street

69 Away From Parking Garage

19 Toward A Building

69 Parking Garage

31 Turning Onto An Island

Ramp

Parking Garage

19 Toward A Building

69 Parking Garage

TRACKING NOTES   Date: 8/23/00 ✓ AM ☐ PM ✓ Day ☐ Night   Dog: Ace, Border Collie
Location: State Park recreation area
Area Description: open-sided buildings
Tracklayer: Heather Jones   Handler: Suzie Smith   TL Started: 7:35am   Dog Started: 10:05am
Ground Conditions: dry   Weather Conditions: hot, humid   Wind Spd: 20mph   Temp: 88°
Components Utilized: 01, 06, 19, 23, 32, 67
Surfaces: grass   asphalt   dirt   concrete   gravel   _____
Articles: ✓Fabric ✓Leather   ✓Plastic ✓Metal
Comments: T1 - No problems with multiple transitions. Ace was fascinated with the inside of the covered building and searched every corner before indicating track direction.   T2 - Blowing dirt from road reduced visibility and pushed scent outside of the building where Ace paralleled on the mulch. Crossed final leg and went to article.

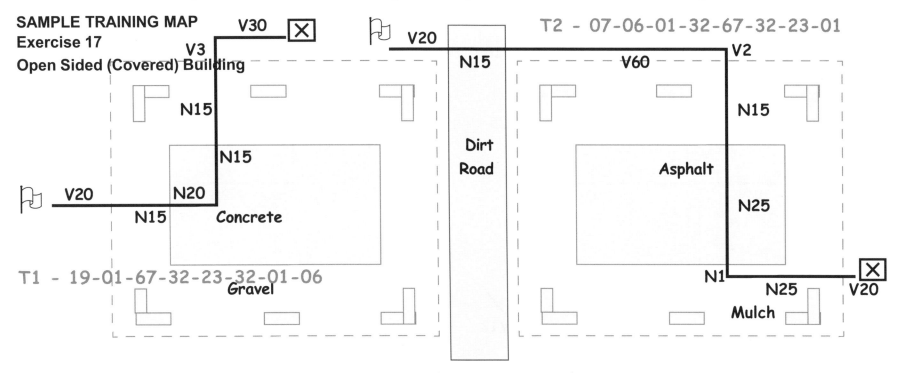

SAMPLE TRAINING MAP
Exercise 17
Open Sided (Covered) Building

TRACKING NOTES

Date: 9/02/00 ✓ AM ☐ PM ✓ Day ☐ Night   Dog: Ace, Border Collie
Location: Shasta County Park Pavillion
Area Description: Open sided metal roofed rodeo arena
Tracklayer: Bob Smith   Handler: Suzie Smith   TL Started: 8:15am   Dog Started:11:40am
Ground Conditions: dry   Weather Conditions: hot   Wind Spd: 4mph   Temp: 92°
Components Utilized: 01, 06, 12, 17, 19, 23, 32, 35, 37, 67
Surfaces: grass   asphalt   mulch   sand   dirt   _____
Articles: ✓Fabric   ✓Leather   ✓Plastic   ✓Metal
Comments: Lethargic tracking in oppressive heat. 10+ degree temperature change under pavillion, marked difference in tracking style from bright sun to covered shade. Numerous new smells distracted Ace; this will be a good proofing exercise to repeat, got lots of practice on "Leave it!" By T3 Ace made a good attempt at making the actual corner.

SAMPLE TRAINING MAP

Exercise 17

Pavilions

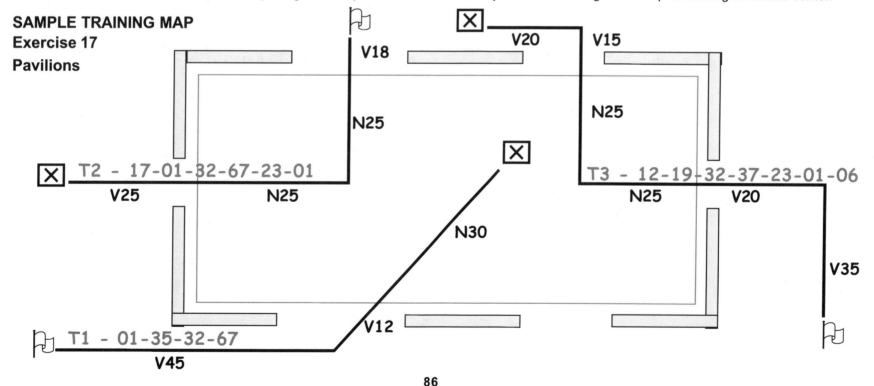

TRACKING NOTES

Date: 9/09/00 ✓ AM ☐ PM ✓ Day ☐ Night   Dog: Ace, Border Collie
Location: County Commissioner's Complex (Parking garages)
Area Description: mowed lawns, sidewalks, asphalt streets, multi-story open-sided parking garages
Tracklayer: Heather Jones   Handler: Suzie Smith   TL Started: 7:30am   Dog Started: 9:15am
Ground Conditions: low grass, dry   Weather Conditions: partly cloudy   Wind Spd: 12mph   Temp: 86°
Components Utilized: 01, 06, 07, 19, 23, 30, 32, 60, 69
Surfaces: grass   asphalt   cement   mulch   dirt _____
Articles: ✓Fabric   ✓Leather   ✓Plastic   ✓Metal
Comments: T1 - Overshot turn. T2 - Lots of casting in garage due to swirling winds, missing article; Ace tried to enter 2nd garage rather than working across street. T3 & T4 - Winds appeared to move scent 10-15 yds in garage. He appears to be getting stronger in garages but still needs lots more work.

SAMPLE TRAINING MAP
Exercise 17

Parking Garages

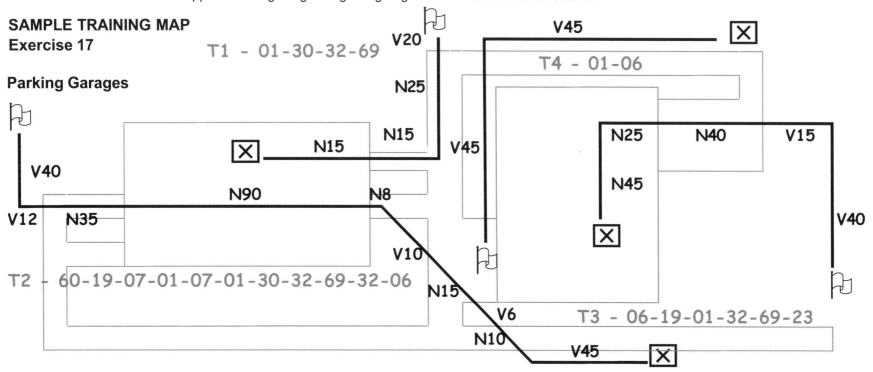

■ **Advanced Training - Incorporating Automobile Components**
■ **Exercise 18**

Exercise	18 - Incorporating Automobile Components
Location	Streets and parking lots
Type of Location	Business/Industrial Park, Campus, School or Church, Office Building
Surfaces	Multiple
Components	As selected
Lesson Plan	Lay the components selected as diagramed. Continue to work the components in this exercise until your dog is confident working these scenting and surface transition problems and you are becoming comfortable with reading your dog's track indications.
Comments	Start yardage should be a minimum of 20 yards to transition area or turn. Continue all legs a minimum of 10 yards past transition areas or turns before ending the exercise.

Always be alert for moving traffic in these areas; and expect to find some or all of your articles left in this area either moved or missing. Watch for oil, antifreeze, or other dangerous substances which may have leaked onto the surface. As a handler you should always be observant and a team member in assisting your dog in the search for articles. Your dog may be required to work around vehicles which have parked on the track or may have parked over an article. Vehicles moving along the track may swirl or disperse the scent while the heat from recently parked vehicles may collect the scent.

Exercise 18 Incorporating Automobile Components
Diagram

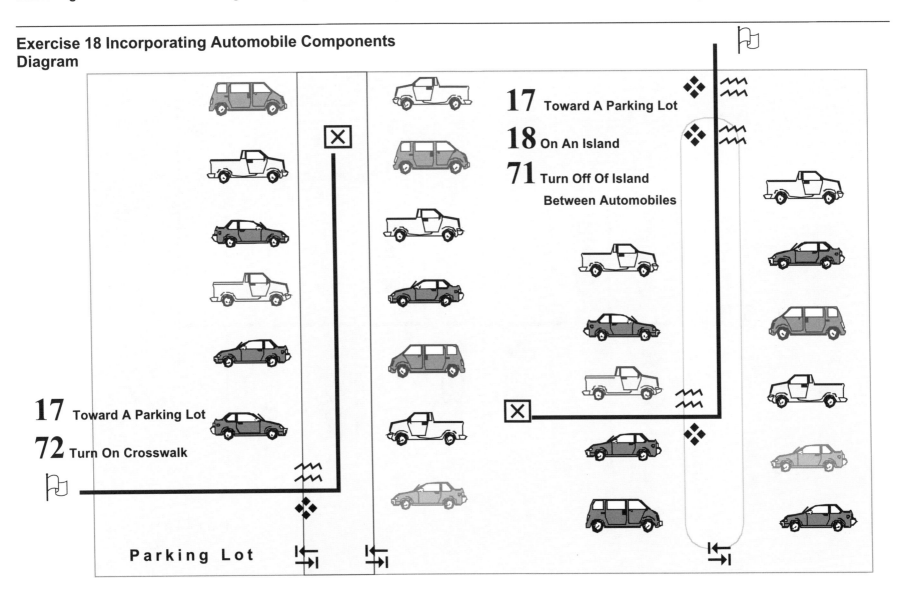

17 Toward A Parking Lot

18 On An Island

71 Turn Off Of Island

Between Automobiles

17 Toward A Parking Lot

72 Turn On Crosswalk

Parking Lot

Exercise 18 Incorporating Automobile Components
Diagram

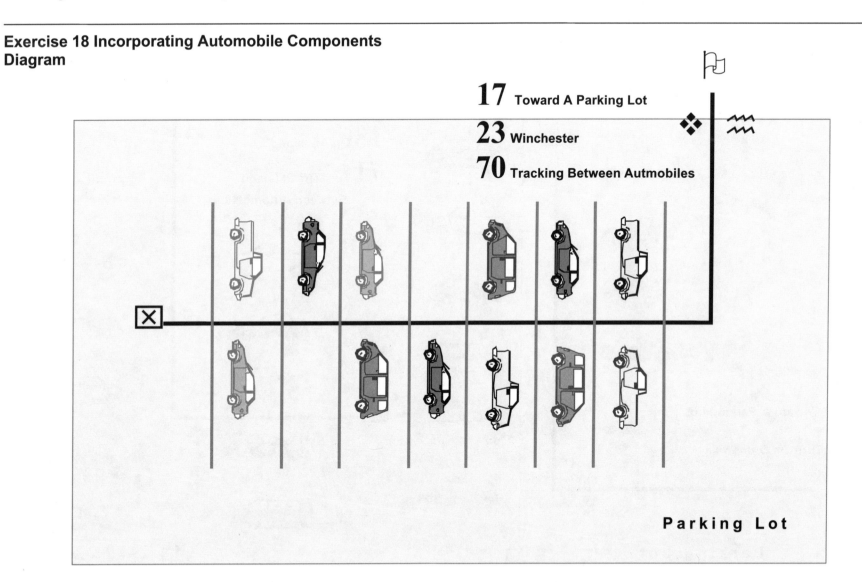

17 Toward A Parking Lot

23 Winchester

70 Tracking Between Autmobiles

Parking Lot

TRACKING NOTES

Date: 9/15/00 ✓ AM ☐ PM ✓ Day ☐ Night   Dog: Ace, Border Collie
Location: City College, Visitor Parking Lot "J
Area Description: asphalt parking lot surrounded by low cut lawn, entry and exit to parking lot is concrete
Tracklayer: Joan Collins   Handler: Suzie Smith   TL Started: 6:20am   Dog Started: 9:38am
Ground Conditions: low grass, dry   Weather Conditions: cloudy   Wind Spd: 2mph   Temp: 77°
Components Utilized: 01, 06, 17, 18, 23, 32, 33, 34, 60, 70, 71, 72
Surfaces: grass   asphalt   mulch   concrete _____ _____
Articles: ✓Fabric ✓Leather   ✓Plastic ✓Metal
Comments: T1 - Indicated NV turn but pushed on to island. Worked around a car and we backed up to the corner.
Took corner, blew through corner on walk, circled car, and came back to track. This is really hard! T2 - Made V cor-
ner, followed curb through corner and around island and then to track!! T3 - No problems. T4 - Overshot turn on
sidewalk, eventually backed up and found track. One more thing to practice!

SAMPLE TRAINING MAP
Exercise 18

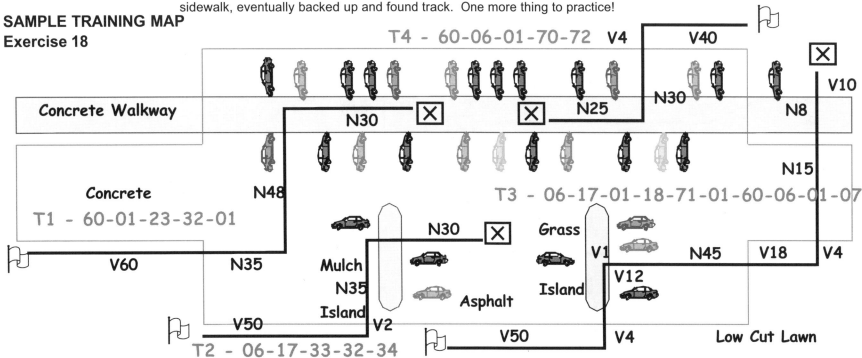

TRACKING NOTES

Date: 9/25/00 ☐ AM ✓ PM ✓ Day ☐ Night   Dog: Ace, Border Collie
Location: City College, Teacher Parking Lot "C"
Area Description: asphalt parking lot surrounded by low cut lawn, entry and exit to parking lot is concrete
Tracklayer: Bob Smith   Handler: Suzie Smith   TL Started: 4:15pm   Dog Started: 5:49pm
Ground Conditions: low grass, dry   Weather Conditions: sunny, hot   Wind Spd: 5mph   Temp: 87°
Components Utilized: 01, 06, 17, 23, 32, 70, 71
Surfaces: grass   asphalt   concrete   _____   _____   _____
Articles: ✓Fabric   ✓Leather   ✓Plastic   ✓Metal
Comments: T1 - Overshot open turn 20 yds, backed up and recovered. T2 - Indicated second corner but went on to curb before coming back. Stepped into PL and met 3 people leaving their cars. Told him to wait, he sat to be petted, and then quickly responded to the re-start routine. T3 - Overshot corner, worked down curb found track in PL! Wow!!

SAMPLE TRAINING MAP
Exercise 18

T1 - 17-06-70

Low Cut Lawn

V50

V5

N65

N45

Concrete

N65

N8

Curb

V8

N75

V30

Asphalt

V40

V50

T2 - 17-06-06-70

T3 - 08-30-70-23-70

Putting It All Together

At this level of your training, you and your dog should be *coming together* as a team. This section will use six imaginary training areas to simulate linking together multiple components into tracks. These areas - Northwest Industrial Park, Southside Business Park, City College, Wayside Elementary School, Wayside High School and Eastside Church are offered as example location you might find in your area for training.

These locations and the size, dimensions and placement of the articles, buildings and roads are for demonstration purposes only. Utilize these examples to help locate training areas and develop tracks for your dog. Track length, article placement and the number of articles utilized in these examples are for training purposes only and may not comply with the regulations. Keep your dog motivated by varying the complexity and length of your training tracks.

As you develop your training tracks remember to establish your article placement as exit routes for each track. If your dog is having a hard time adjusting to the wind conditions, weather or complexity of the track be prepared, at any article, to end the track and switch from training to a play time with your dog.

■ Advanced Training - Integrating Components Into Tracks
■ **Putting It All Together**

Comments   Included are maps of six imaginary training areas to provide you an opportunity to evaluate potential components which may exist within the site. For each of these training areas, included is a series of five sample tracks to give you an example of how you might plot the various components as discussed in this book. The examples as shown are not the only possibilities. In training you may disregard the minimum lengths for legs, numbers of turns, types of surfaces or other variables in order to challenge your dog to problem solve.

The sample tracks are not in compliance with all AKC Regulations nor are they to scale. It is not as important for you to work full length tracks as it is for you to understand the concept of training at the component level and learning to read and understand the subtle indications of your dog. Hopefully at this point in your training you and your dog are starting to work together and as your progression continues you will merge into a working team.

If possible, locate training sites within your geographic area which contain similar features. Utilize the concepts in these sample tracks and the component examples contained within this book to expand the possibilities of your training sites.

As with any training, be considerate of the property owners by keeping your dog out of the flowers and picking up behind him.

Sample Locations
- Northwest Industrial Park
- Southside Business Park
- City College
- Wayside Elementary School
- Wayside High School
- Eastside Church

Northwest Industrial Park

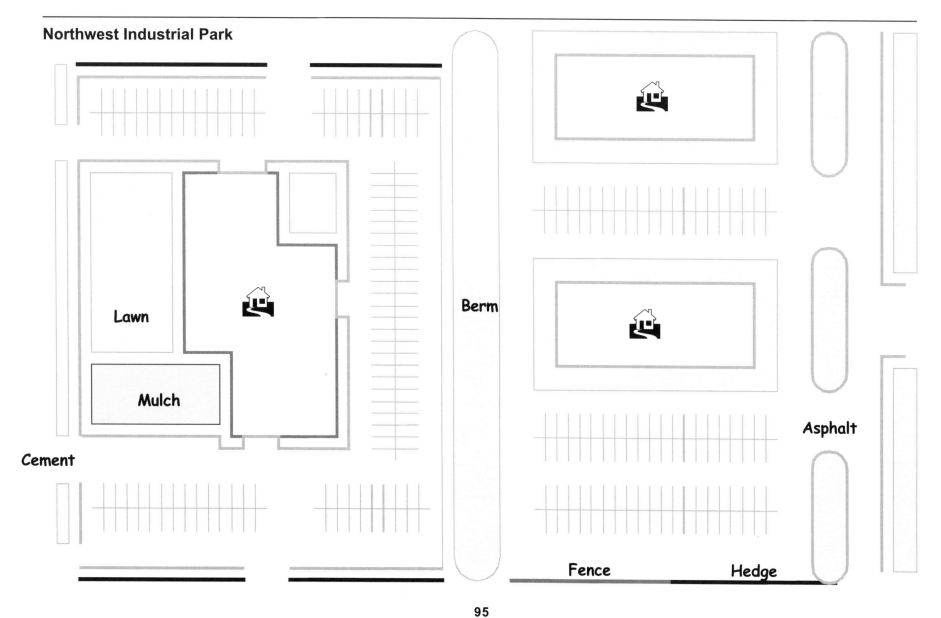

Northwest Industrial Park

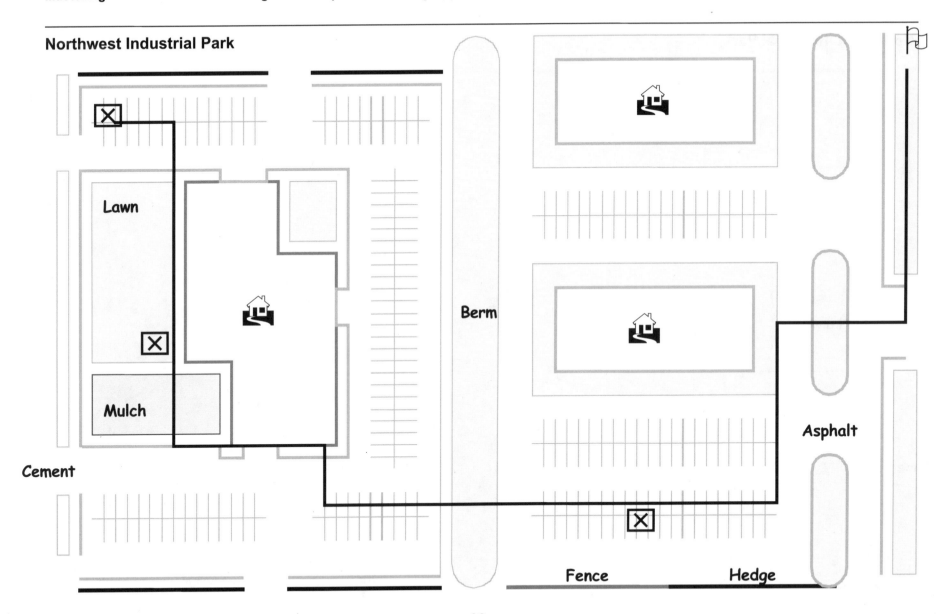

Lawn

Mulch

Cement

Berm

Asphalt

Fence

Hedge

Northwest Industrial Park

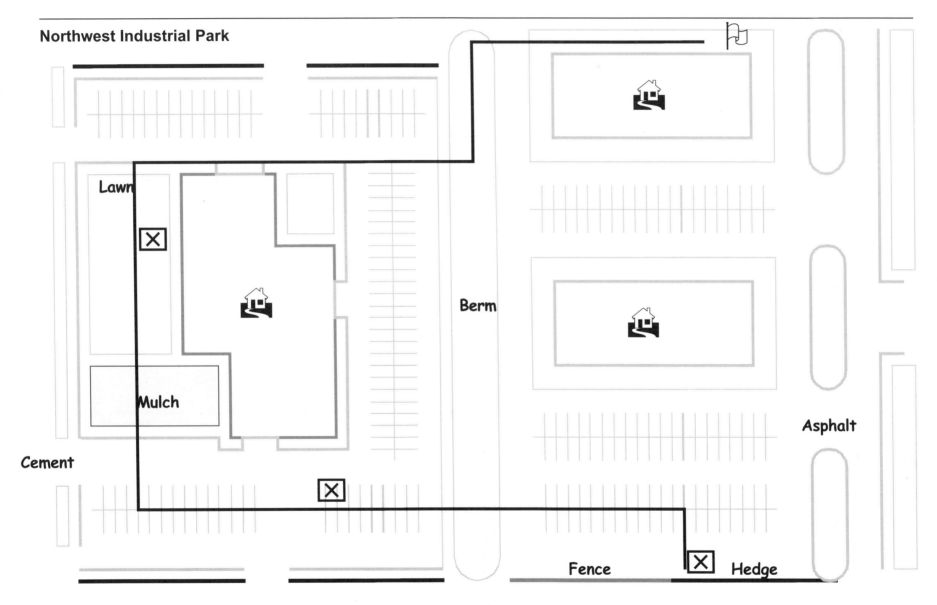

Lawn

Mulch

Berm

Cement

Asphalt

Fence   Hedge

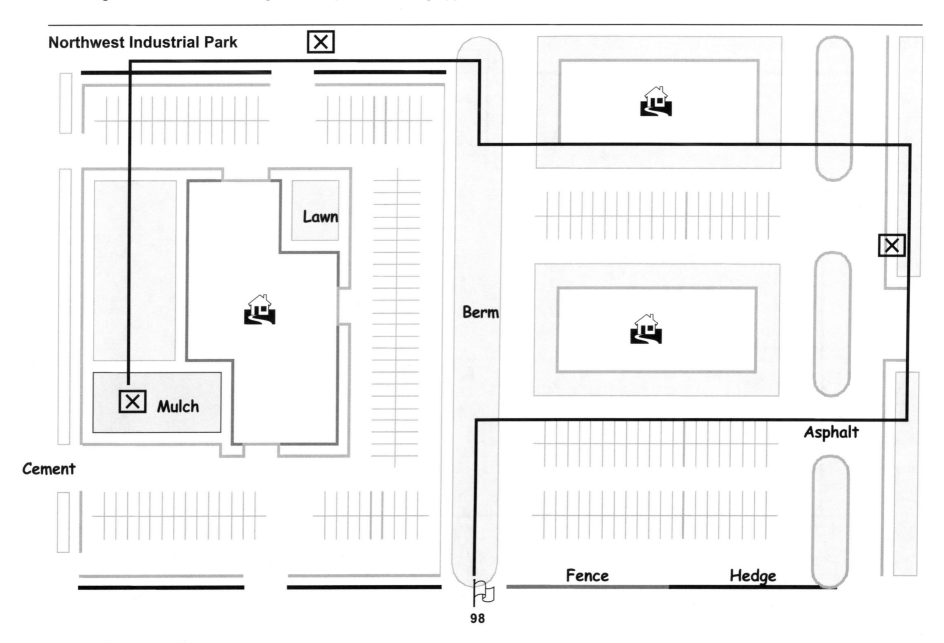

Northwest Industrial Park

Lawn

Berm

Mulch

Cement

Asphalt

Fence   Hedge

98

Northwest Industrial Park

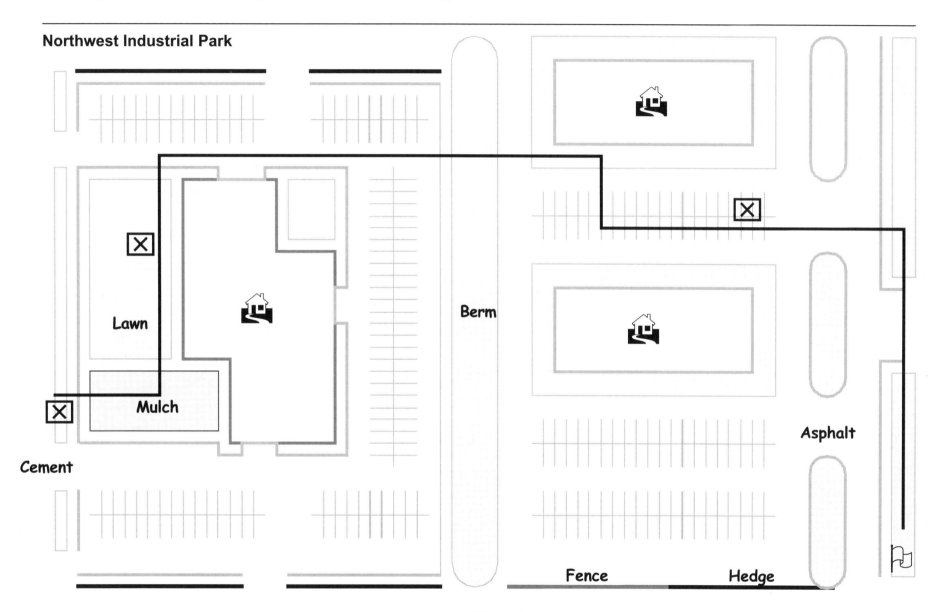

Berm

Lawn

Mulch

Cement

Asphalt

Fence   Hedge

Northwest Industrial Park

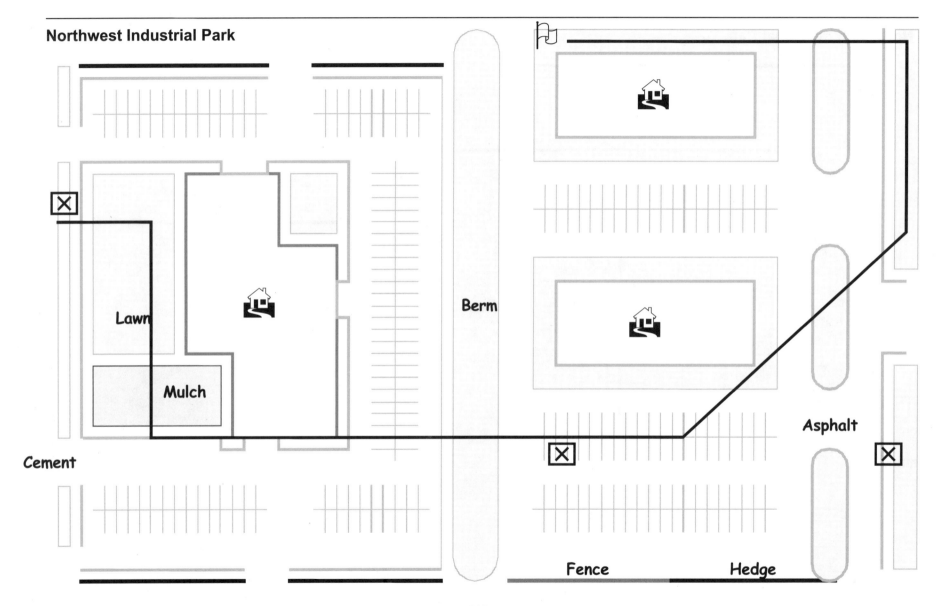

Lawn

Mulch

Cement

Berm

Asphalt

Fence

Hedge

Southside Business Park

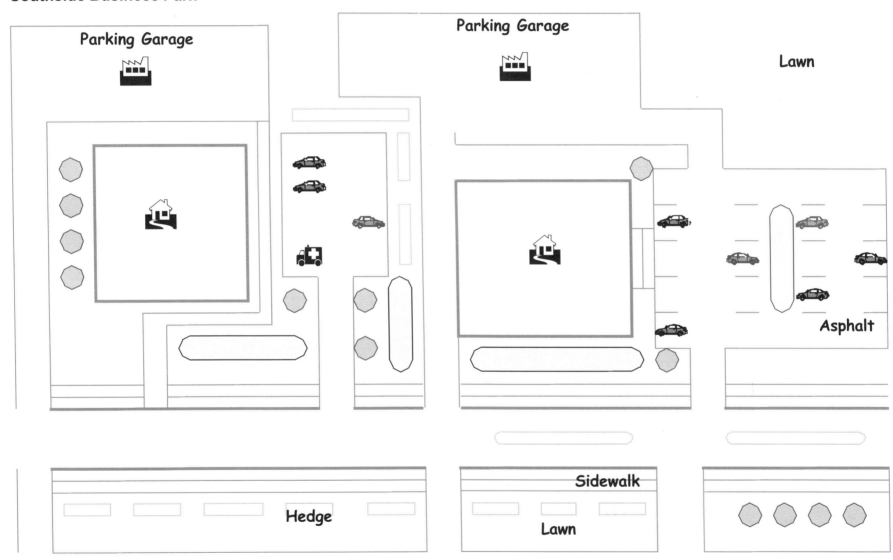

Southside Business Park

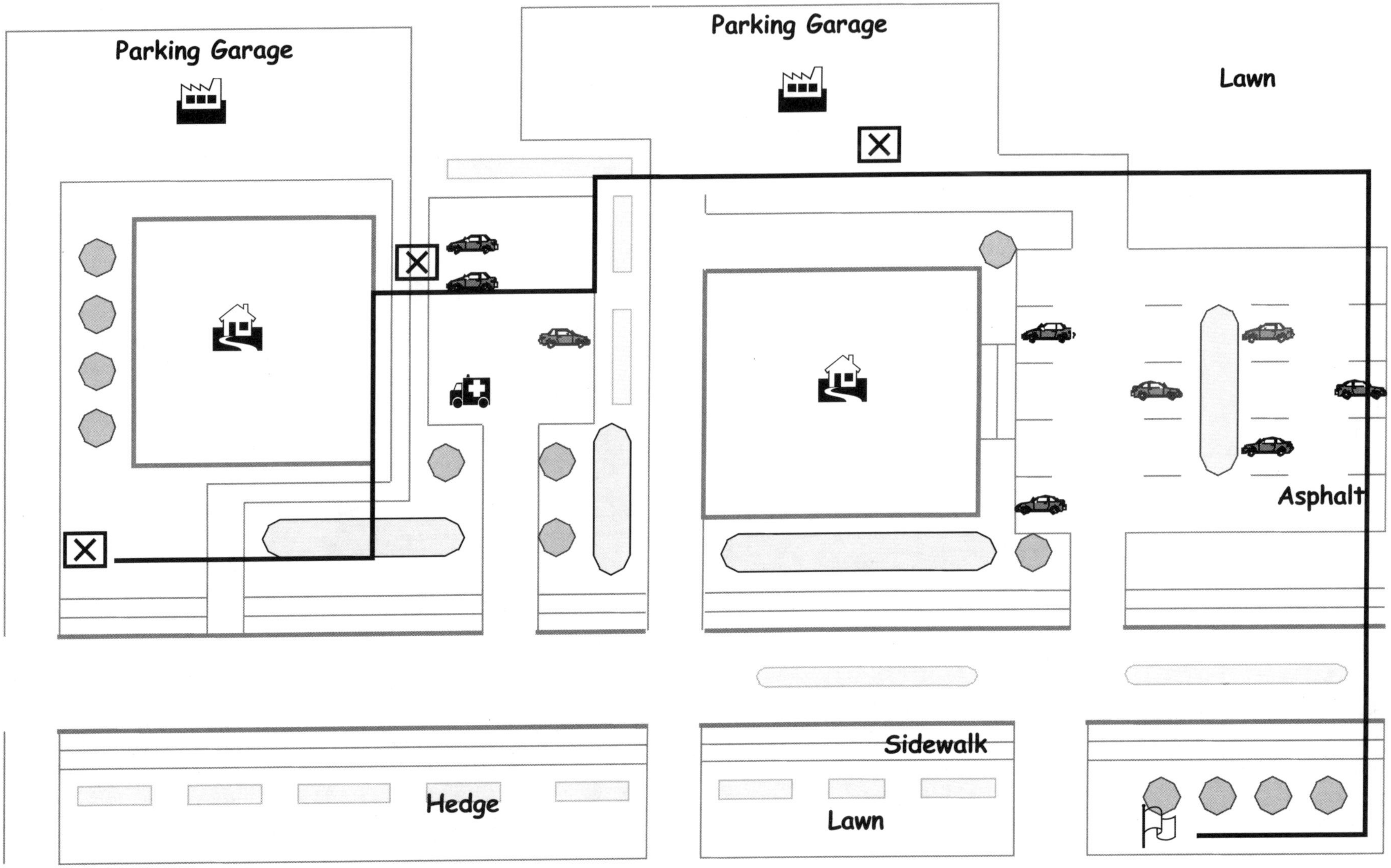

Parking Garage

Parking Garage

Lawn

Asphalt

Sidewalk

Hedge

Lawn

Southside Business Park

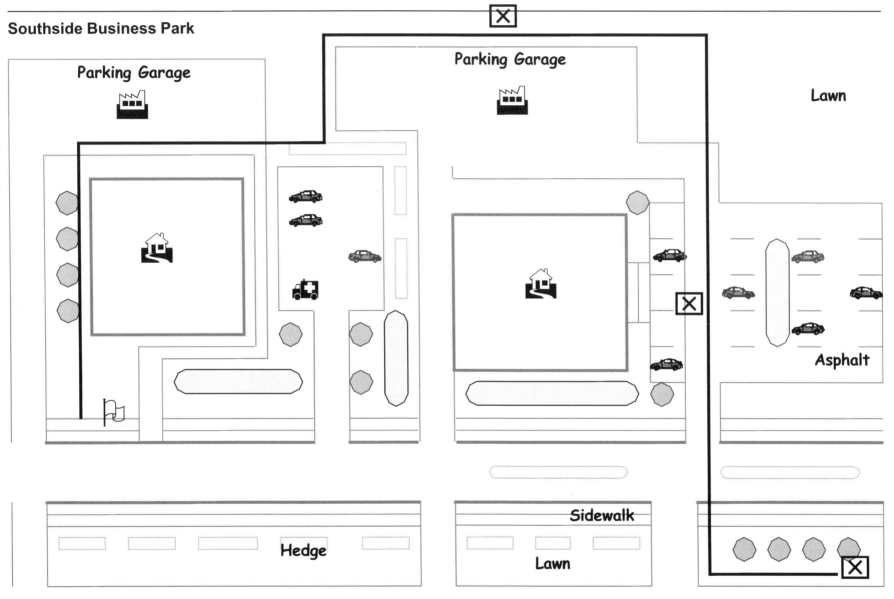

Southside Business Park

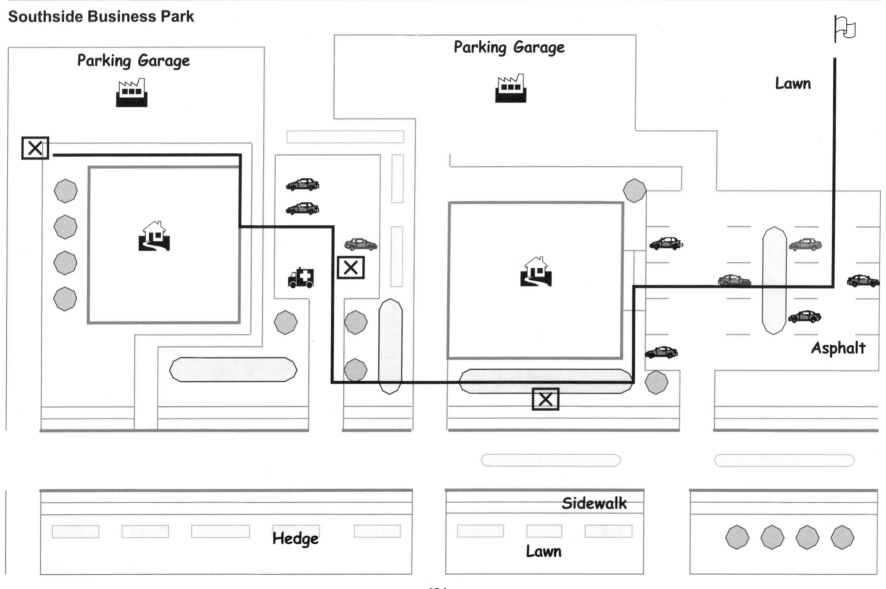

Southside Business Park

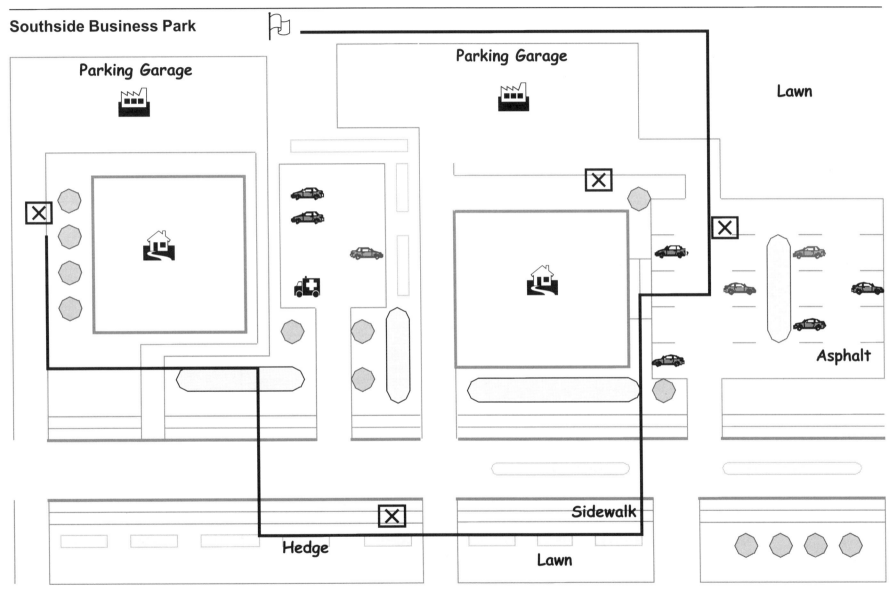

Southside Business Park

City College

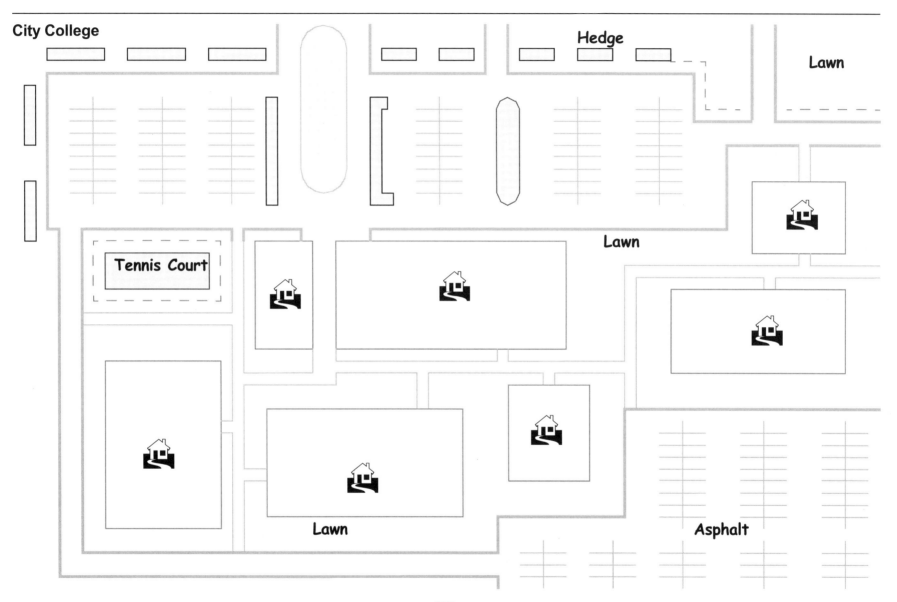

Hedge

Lawn

Lawn

Tennis Court

Lawn

Asphalt

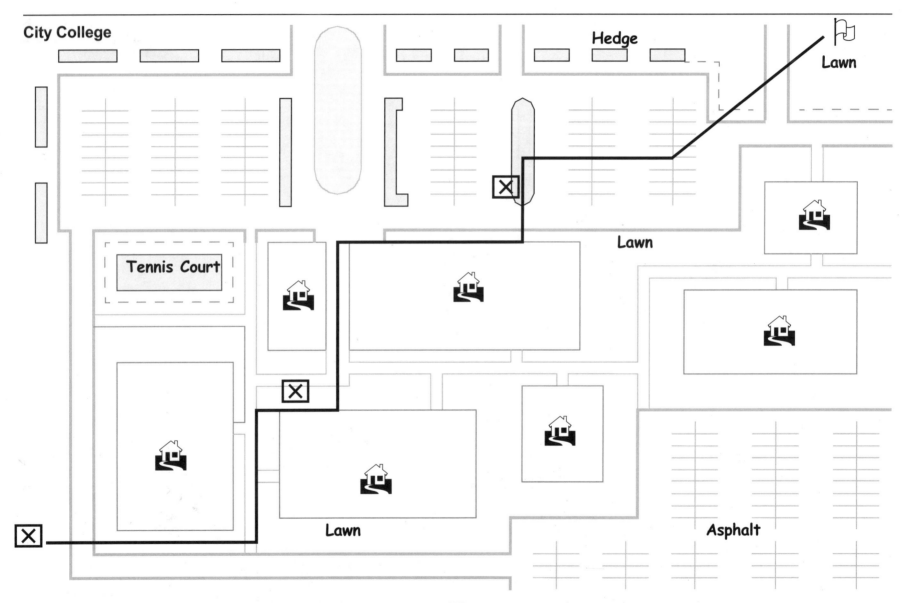

City College

Hedge

Lawn

Tennis Court

Lawn

Lawn

Asphalt

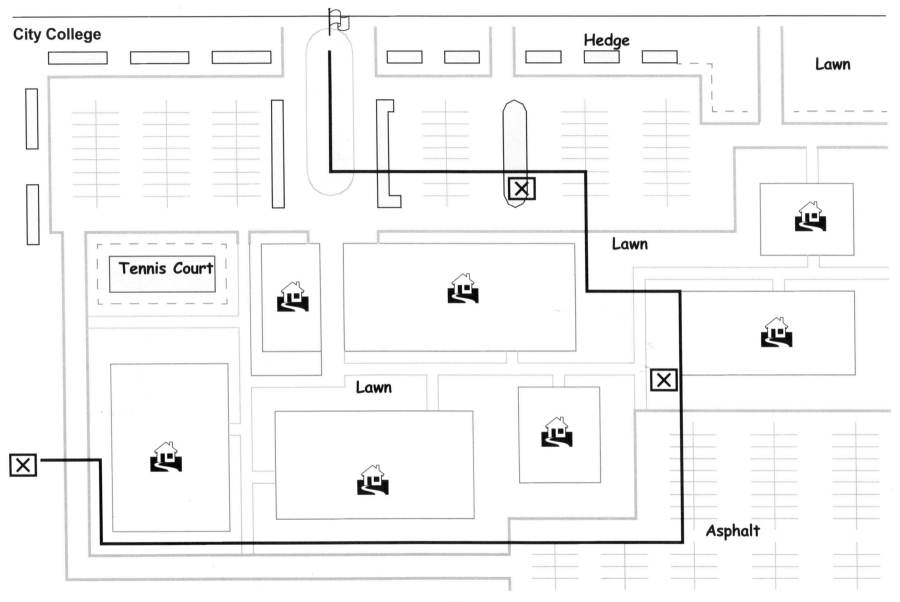

City College

Hedge

Lawn

Lawn

Tennis Court

Lawn

Asphalt

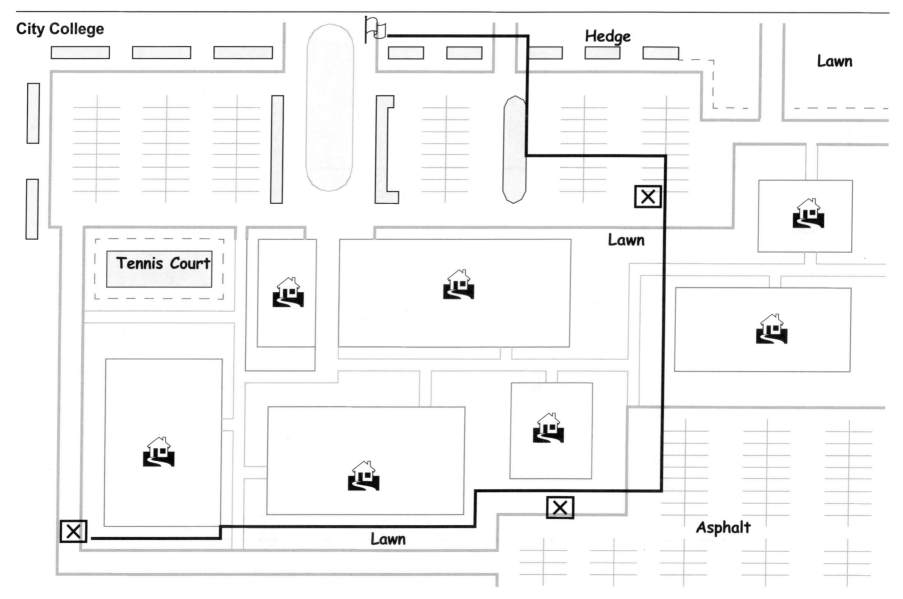

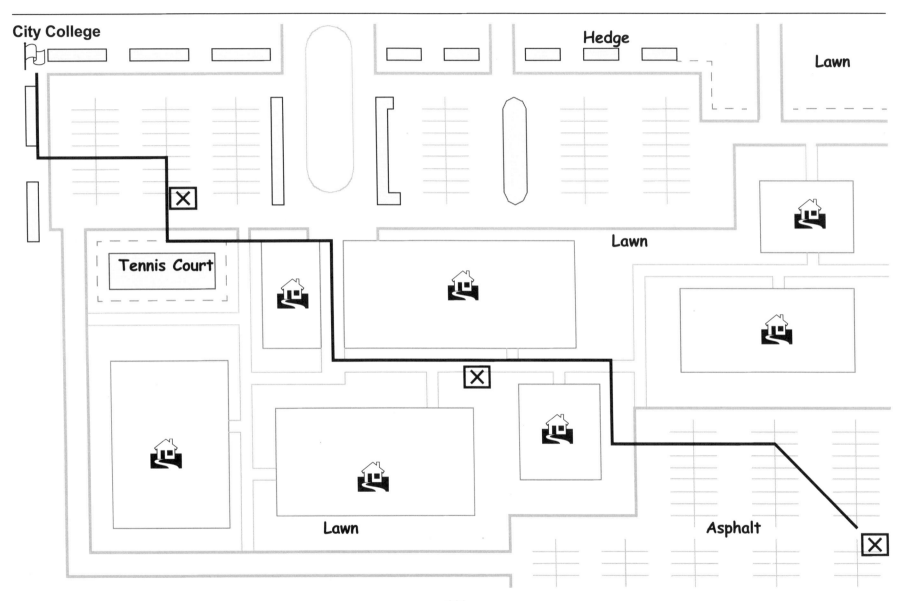

City College

Hedge

Lawn

Tennis Court

Lawn

Lawn

Lawn

Asphalt

City College

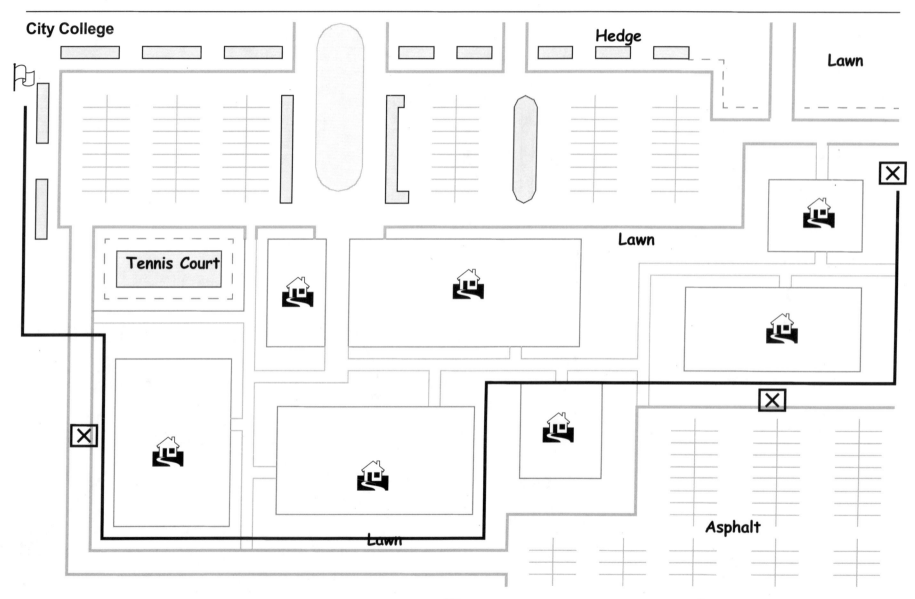

Hedge

Lawn

Tennis Court

Lawn

Lawn

Asphalt

Wayside Elementary School

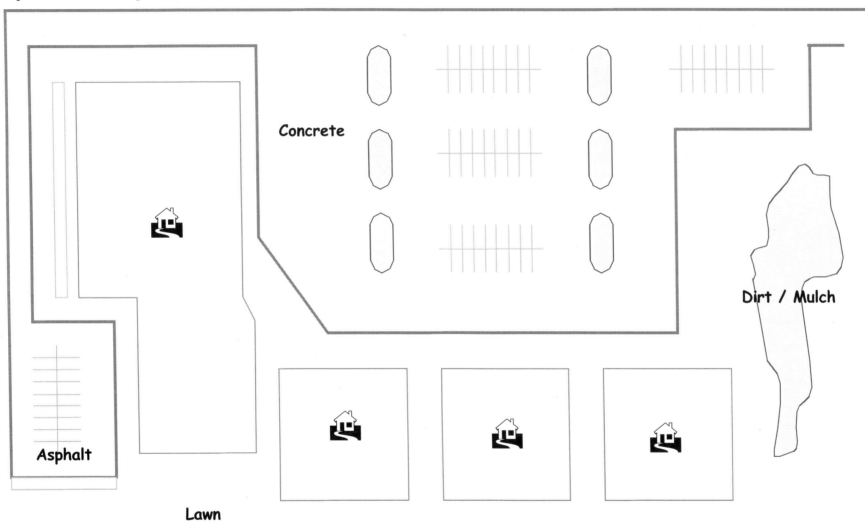

Concrete

Dirt / Mulch

Asphalt

Lawn

Wayside Elementary School

Concrete

Dirt / Mulch

Asphalt

Lawn

Wayside Elementary School

Concrete

Dirt / Mulch

Asphalt

Lawn

Wayside Elementary School

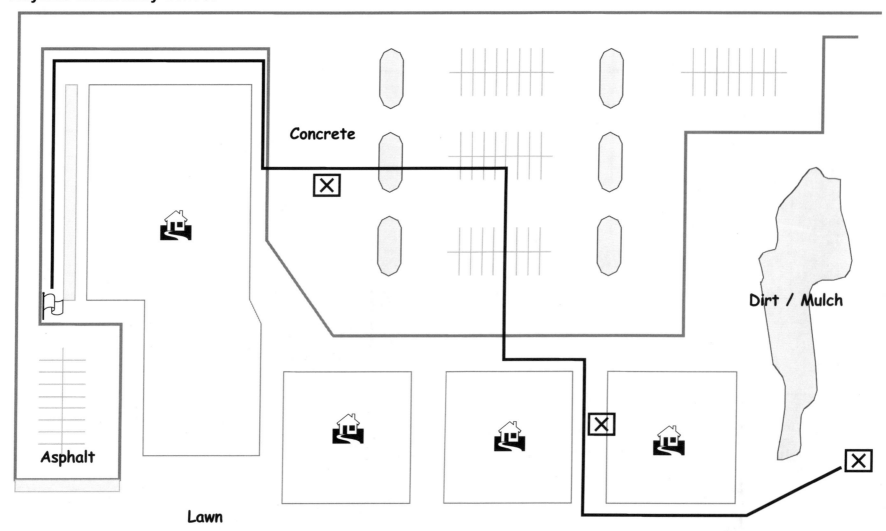

Concrete

Dirt / Mulch

Asphalt

Lawn

Wayside Elementary School

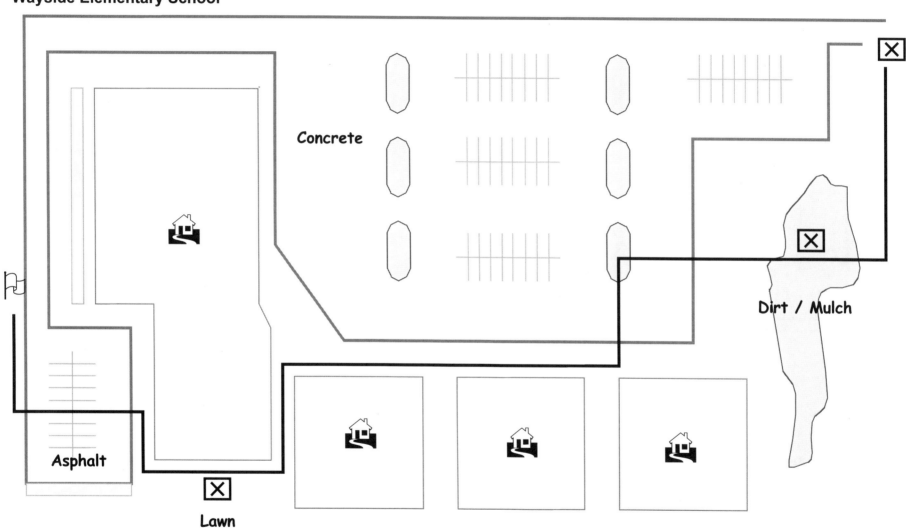

Wayside Elementary School

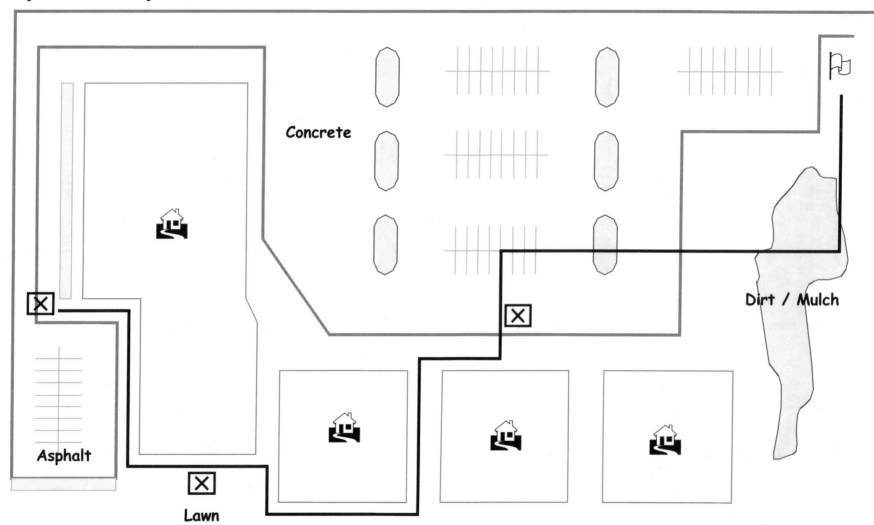

Wayside High School

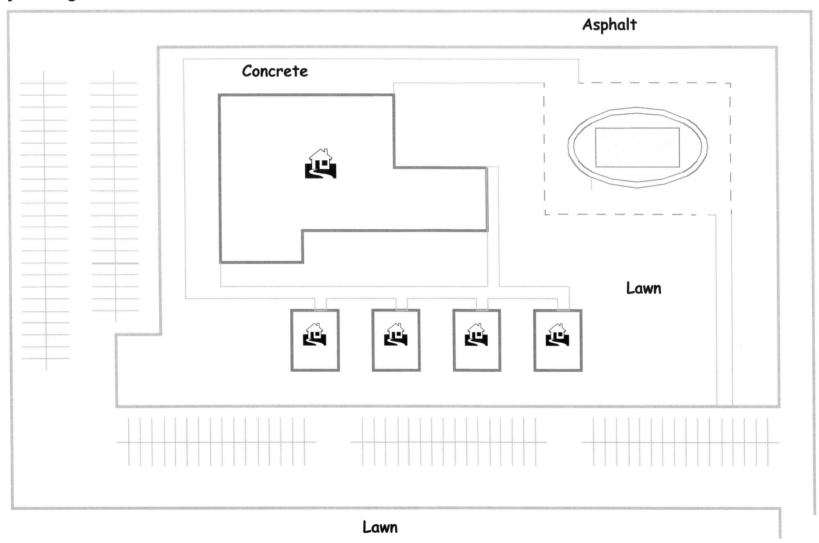

Wayside High School

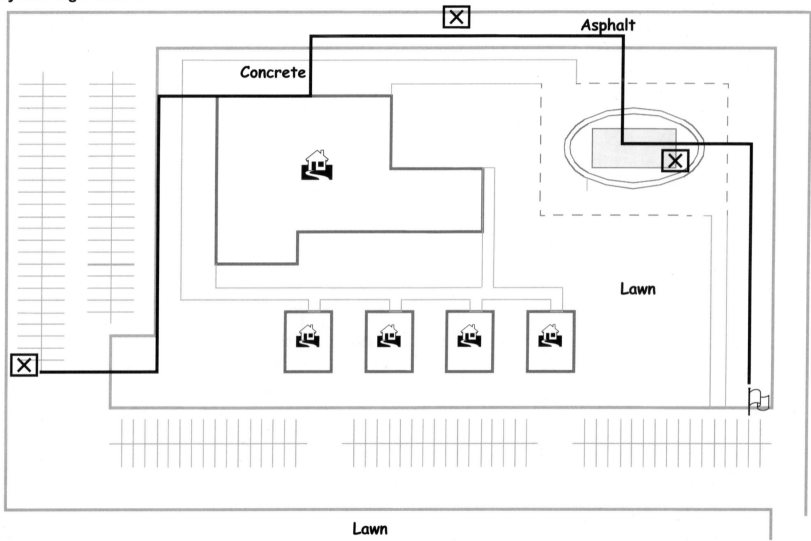

Wayside High School

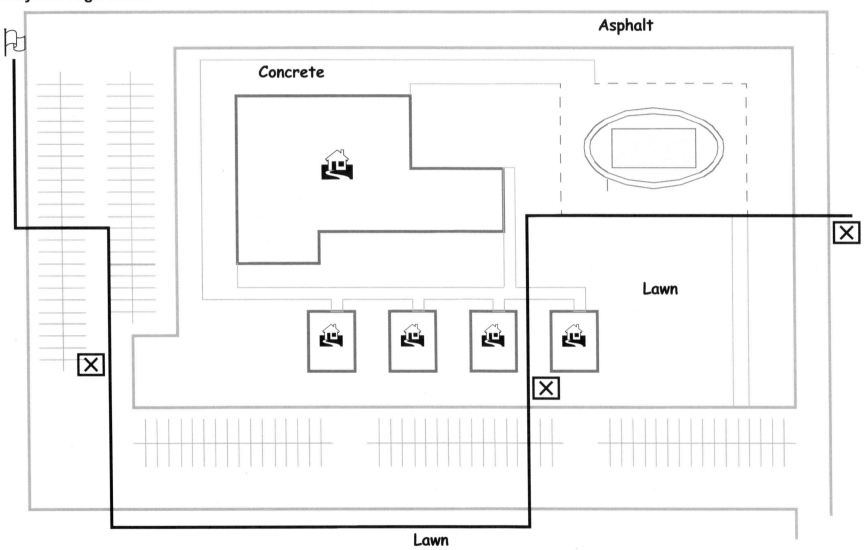

Asphalt

Concrete

Lawn

Lawn

Wayside High School

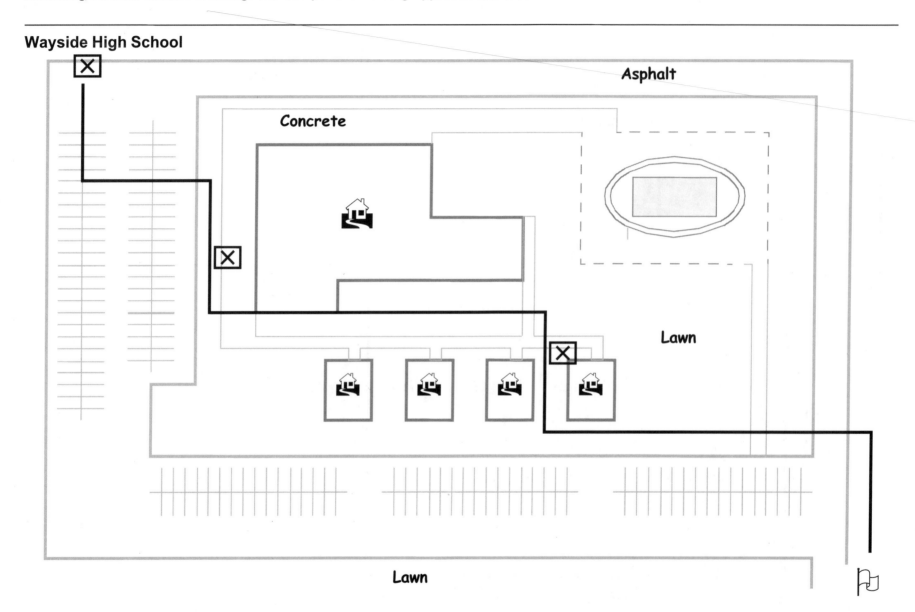

Wayside High School

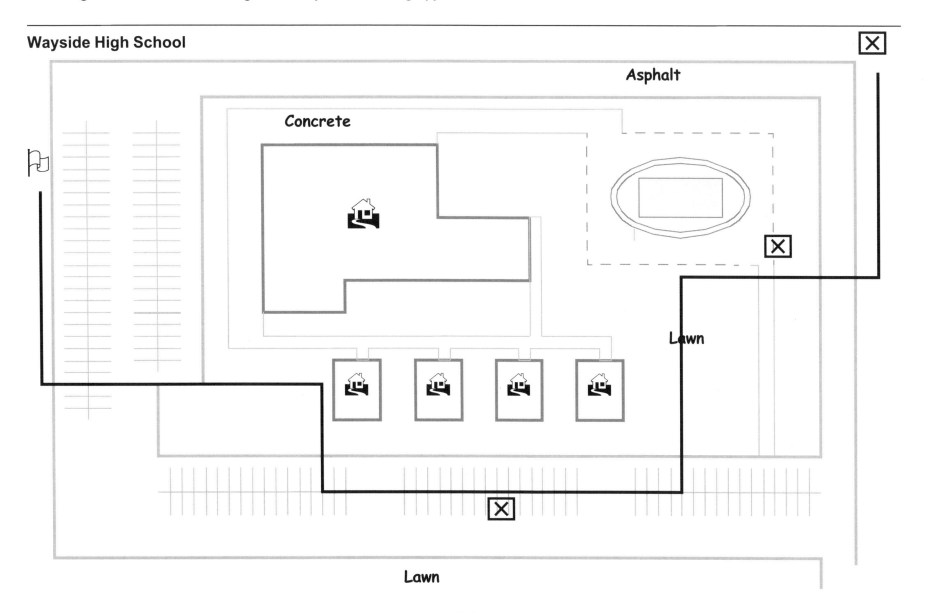

Wayside High School

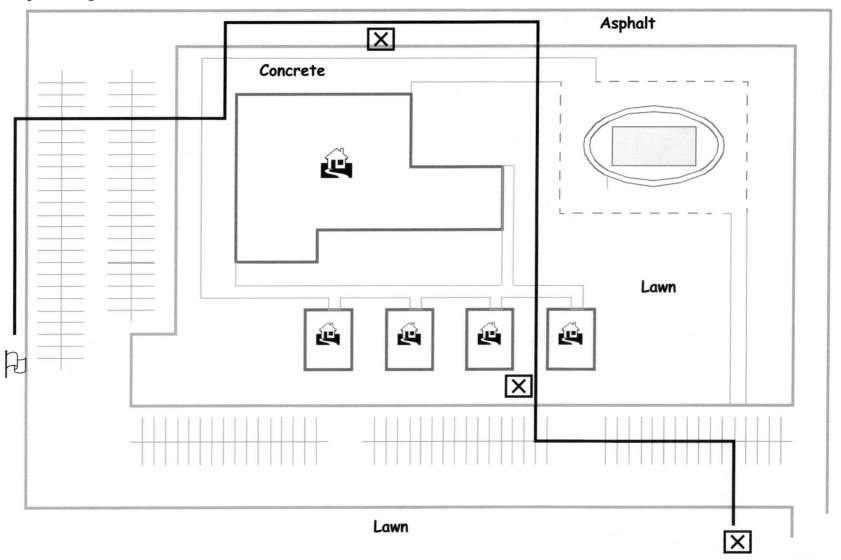

Eastside Church

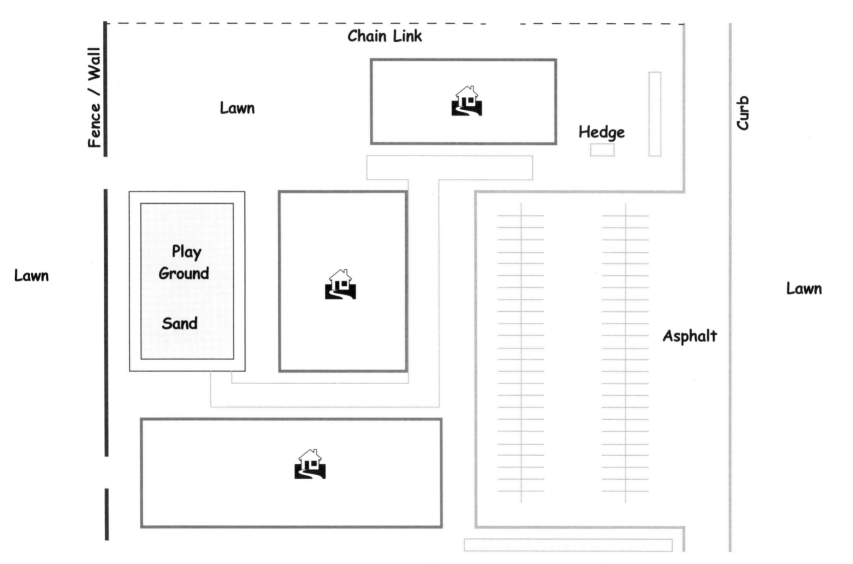

Eastside Church

Eastside Church

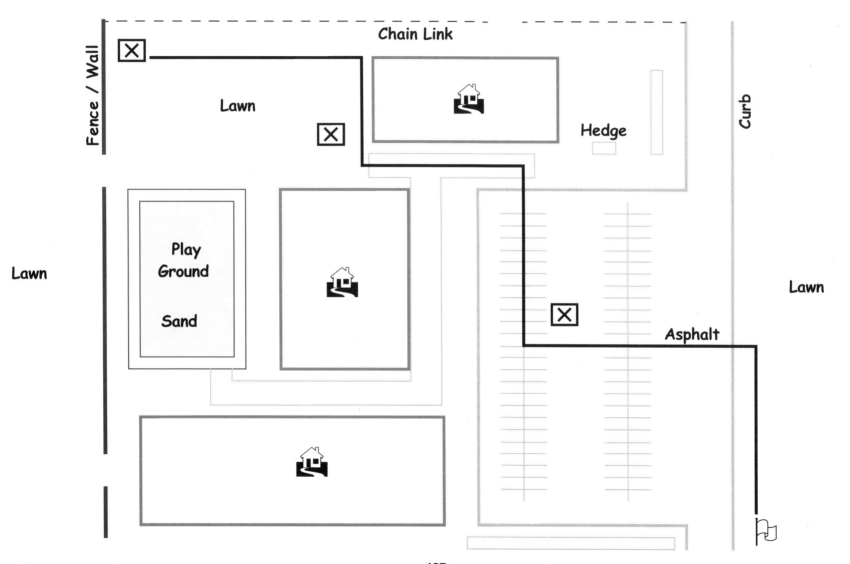

Eastside Church

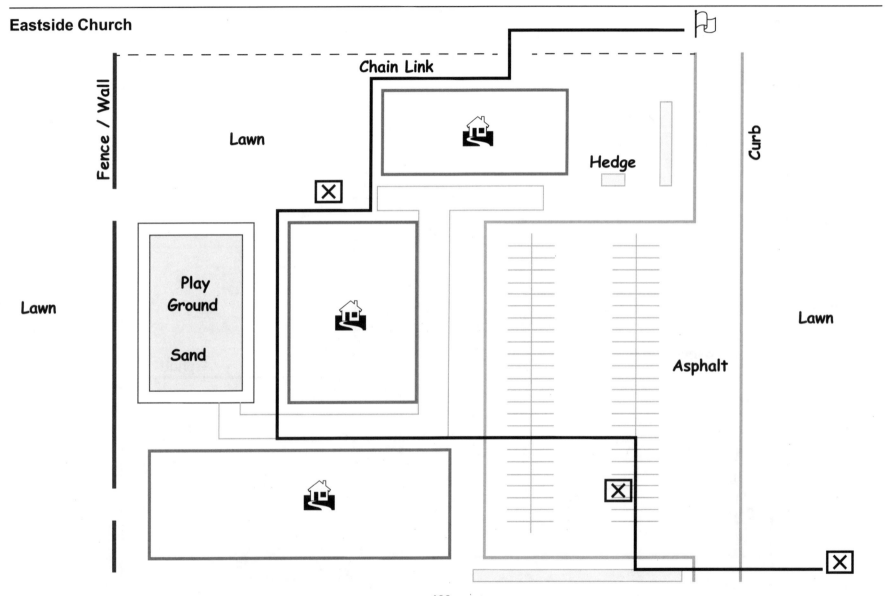

128

Eastside Church

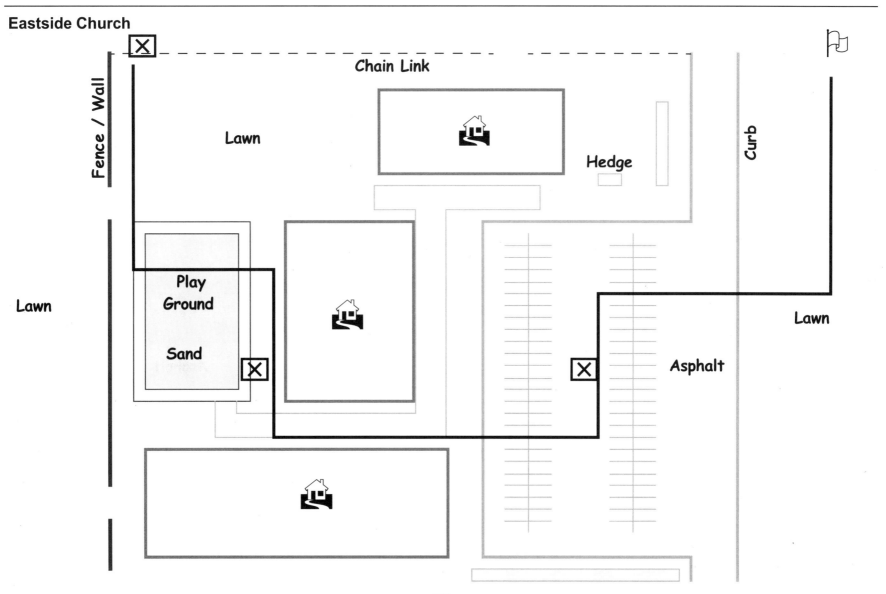

Eastside Church

Index by Subject